IMAGES
of America

REYNOLDSBURG AND TRURO TOWNSHIP

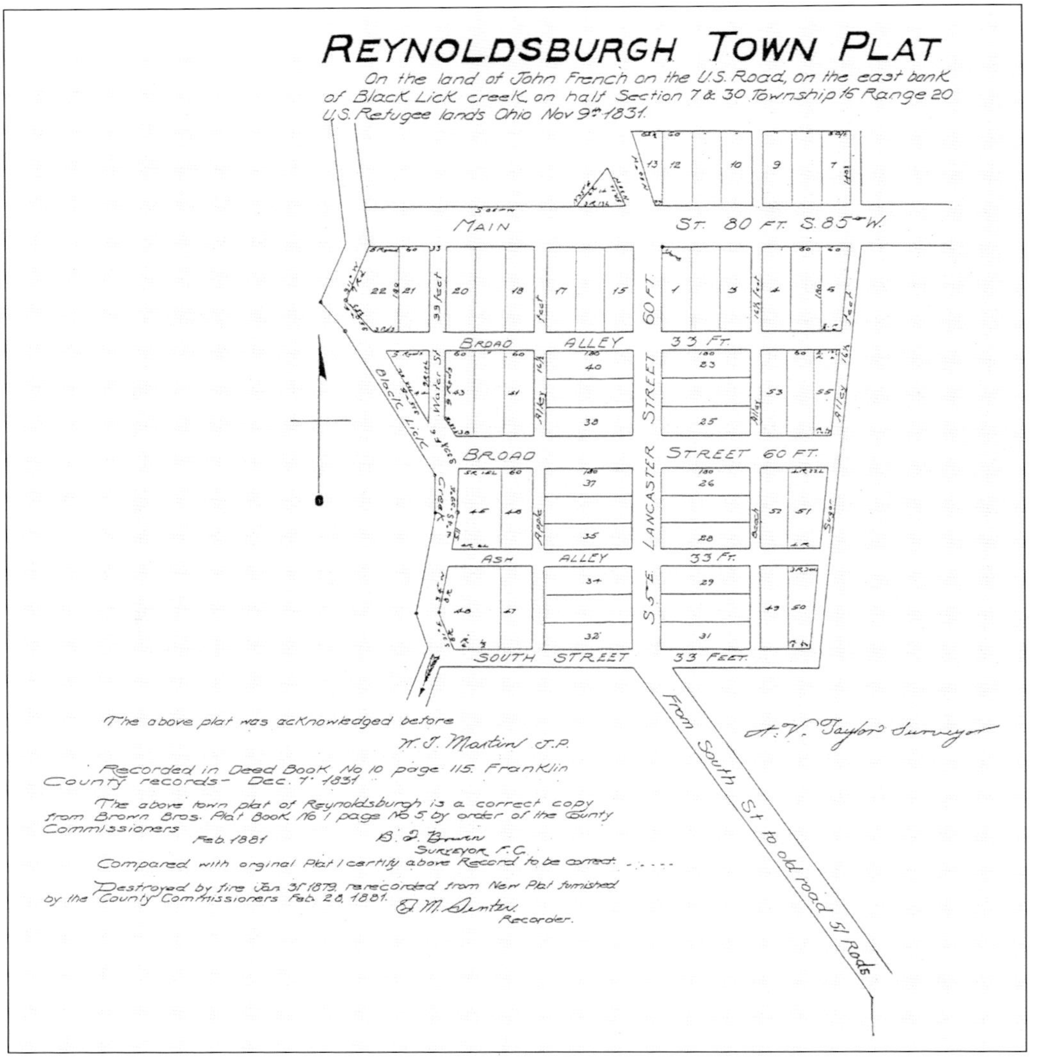

1831 Reynoldsburgh Plat Map. This map was created by Abiather Vinton Taylor, who surveyed the farmland of John D. French so it could be sectioned into parcels for the village of Reynoldsburgh. (Courtesy of Cornelia M. Parkinson.)

On the Cover: 1932 Washington Bicentennial Celebration. The entire town of Reynoldsburg gathered on the front lawn of the Reynoldsburg School to celebrate the Fourth of July 1932 Washington bicentennial. They sat for the photographer while he took a panoramic photograph. The central figure (in a white shirt and tie) is James A. Oppy (1872–1956), superintendent of the Reynoldsburg School from 1929 to 1944. (Courtesy of the Reynoldsburg-Truro Historical Society.)

IMAGES
of America

REYNOLDSBURG AND TRURO TOWNSHIP

Mary Turner Stoots
with Cornelia M. Parkinson

ARCADIA
PUBLISHING

ISBN 978-1-4671-0736-5

Published by Arcadia Publishing
Charleston, South Carolina

Printed in the United States of America

Library of Congress Control Number: 2021950576

For all general information, please contact Arcadia Publishing:
Telephone 843-853-2070
Fax 843-853-0044
E-mail sales@arcadiapublishing.com
For customer service and orders:
Toll-Free 1-888-313-2665

Visit us on the Internet at www.arcadiapublishing.com

To all who have a passion for learning more about our local history

Contents

Acknowledgments		6
Introduction		7
1.	Early Settlers	9
2.	Religious Freedom and Freedom from Slavery	17
3.	Families and Homes	27
4.	Schools	45
5.	Community Involvement	65
6.	Street Scenes and Landmarks	81
7.	Agriculture and Business	89
8.	Notable People from Truro Township	101

Acknowledgments

Twenty-two interested people met at Graham Road School on April 30, 1975, to discuss the idea of forming a Reynoldsburg-area historical society. Temporary officers and committee members served until the first annual meeting in September 1975. Following the Ohio State Historical Society guidelines, the committee drew up a constitution.

A thank-you goes to Caitrin Cunningham, senior title manager at Arcadia Publishing, for patiently answering all of our questions and offering words of encouragement. A thank-you as well to the Reynoldsburg-Truro Historical Society (abbreviated as RTHS in this book's courtesy lines) for opening their archives, searching their files, and sharing their collections, specifically the Cornelia M. Parkinson photograph collection and the McNaghten Collection by Eleanor Wilson Shonting.

Over time, hundreds of people have donated their free time to volunteer at the museum. There are too many to list them all individually, but without the help of a core group, this book would not have been possible.

We would like to thank the following in alphabetical order: Linda Bronstein, Martha Ashton Brown, Charity Connell, Jim and Judy Diuguid, Regina Haft, Sylvia Tussing Hering, Carolyn Ashton Hill, Dianne Foltz Hoffman, Suzy Millar Miller, Marvin D. Shrimplin, Phillip Thomas, and David Windom.

A special thank-you goes to Mark Myers for transporting boxes of photographs from the museum to the author's house for scanning and spending countless hours searching through the vertical files. The volunteers who maintain the museum collections have earned our immeasurable gratitude.

INTRODUCTION

It was just past 1800 when James and Martha Crawford and Thomas Palmer were arriving in the area now known as Reynoldsburg and Truro Township. Ohio was still a wilderness inhabited by wild things—wolves, panthers, beaver, a very few bison and bear, elk, deer, and foxes of red, grey, and black. Great flocks of birds darkened the skies—ducks, geese, turkeys, pigeons, pileated and ivory-billed woodpeckers, and native swans. And there were snakes—thousands of snakes; poisonous, nonpoisonous, aggressive, retiring, huge, and small, the snakes were everywhere in the forests, waters, and sunny meadows of the new state.

The indigenous peoples of the area were more fearsome than the wild animals, for they had animal cunning, a broad knowledge of their own terrain, and the human ability to think and outthink and to kill, steal, or mutilate hapless settlers. They often showed friendship and generosity to the white usurpers of the territory their people had inhabited for centuries, but the new arrivals had no way of knowing if the indigenous peoples who came to Blacklick Creek and Big Walnut Creek to hunt and crack flint were hostile or not until—for a few—it was too late.

Many of the people who forced the indigenous tribes off the land were recognized as adventurers in the finest sense of the word. Some were heroes of the American Revolution, with their no less heroic wives and families. Some came from cities, where their everyday lives included leather-bound books and satin breeches and the theater and fine houses with genuine glass in all the windows. There were farmers and farm wives accustomed to unrelenting labor and with a yearning to see a new part of their country. There were the educated, and those whose fingers found gripping a pen strange. There were good men and bad and those who straddled the law, but the best of them were men and women of incredible bravery and fairness and concern for their neighbors.

Many of them journeyed from Scotland. In that country, one was either Catholic or belonged to the National Church of Scotland (Presbyterian). The Presbyterians came to America to escape persecution from the Catholics. Some landed in Truro, Nova Scotia, when arriving on this continent.

The refugees from Scotland fought for the Americans during the Revolutionary War, and the federal government could not afford to pay in dollars but instead gave them land. The Continental Congress was formed in 1774. The Revolutionary War ended in 1783. In 1783, land was promised to the Scottish refugees, and in 1785, Congress passed a resolution regarding land grants to refugees from Nova Scotia and devised a method of surveying land into squares for disbursement. In 1789, George Washington was inaugurated as the first president of the United States, and by 1798, Congress had passed an act providing for the filing of claims to the refugee lands in this area. Reynoldsburg sits in the center of the four-county Refugee Tract. It starts at the Scioto River, is 4.5 miles wide and 48 miles long, and ends in Licking and Perry Counties.

The Pilgrims brought the township form of government to the New World in 1620. In Ohio, the township form predates the state government. The size and shape of the township was determined by the Congressional acts establishing various land grants. All Ohio land grants (except the Virginia Military Lands) were surveyed into townships either five or six miles square under the Range and Township system. In the earliest years of statehood, the Ohio township government cared for the poor, maintained the roads, preserved the peace, registered brands of stock-owners, and in general fulfilled the needs of local government.

Truro Township was established and organized in 1810. It had originally been part of Liberty Township. The first election for Truro Township officers was held at the residence of the Robert Taylor family on Big Walnut Creek. Those attending the meeting elected to name the new township Truro in honor of Truro, Nova Scotia, whence several settlers had come.

In 1813, Daniel Dunihue bought 320 acres in Half-Section 30W from the heirs of Revolutionary War soldier Adam Johnston, which was the eventual site of the village of Reynoldsburg. John D. and Jane Graham French arrived in the fall of 1816 from New York State. John bought land from Daniel Dunihue. By 1816, Truro Township had 260 inhabitants.

The village and township had many churches. Between 1817 and 1836, six churches had been established in Truro Township and three meetinghouses had been erected; the Seceders (United Presbyterian) were first; they organized in 1817 and built their church in 1818. Truro Presbyterian Church was organized and erected a church in 1820. In 1822, the Friendship (Primitive) Baptist Church was formed. In 1828, a Methodist Church Society formed at Brice and started work on a building. The Methodists in Reynoldsburg were organized in 1835 and built a structure in 1836.

Also in 1836, the Reynoldsburg Presbyterian Church was organized. The Presbyterians built in 1840 and the Baptists in about 1843; in 1848, a Universalist church was formed. The Methodist Church Society in Brice became the Society of Powell's Chapel in 1850; the following year, they built a meetinghouse. The Baptists dismantled their first church, cleaned the brick and added more, and built a second one about 1860. The next year, the Presbyterian church burned and was rebuilt from the ground up. The year after that, the United Presbyterians built in the village. In 1870, the Church of Christ (Campbellite) was built. The Methodists built a brick church on Main Street in 1871.

In 1830, the National Road was under construction and had finally reached the village. Along with the road came James C. Reynolds from Zanesville, who rented a room from John French. Reynolds promptly built a log structure for use as a sutler's store. Besides having general provisions for sale, this building also served as the post office.

In 1831, French hired Abiather Vinton Taylor to survey his farmland to create a town. Reynolds had clearly developed into a popular figure within the village, because the map Taylor provided was labeled as the "Reynoldsburgh Town Plat."

Reynolds was appointed the first postmaster in 1833 and was later voted by the people to become a brigadier general in the militia and went on to serve a term in the Ohio legislature.

For the next 135 years, Reynoldsburg remained a small village surrounded by farmland. The population grew very slowly, increasing by about 450 persons. The 1950 Census reflected a total of 724 individuals who lived in Reynoldsburg.

By 1960, the village had increased in size by 976.4 percent to a population of 7,793. At one point, advertisements labeled it the "Fastest Growing Town in America." On January 5, 1961, the Ohio secretary of state designated Reynoldsburg as a city.

In this book, the authors' goal is to take readers on a journey from the early days of the settlers and introduce them to the individuals who built this town from the bottom up. These are folks from all walks of life who started small businesses, farmed the fields, policed the streets, taught in the schools, served on the volunteer fire department, ran for office in city government, raised their children here, and worshipped in the churches. Most of them have since been buried in the area's cemeteries.

All of them worked hard to make this town the wonderful city it is today.

One

Early Settlers

Abiather Vinton Taylor. Abiather Vinton Taylor (1783–1853) was born in Truro, Nova Scotia, and was the oldest son of pioneers Robert (1759–1828) and Mehetable (1765–1857) Taylor. In 1831, Abiather surveyed John French's farmland so that a town could be created; he was described as a large, handsome, broad-shouldered, dignified, and kindhearted man. (Courtesy of Cornelia M. Parkinson.)

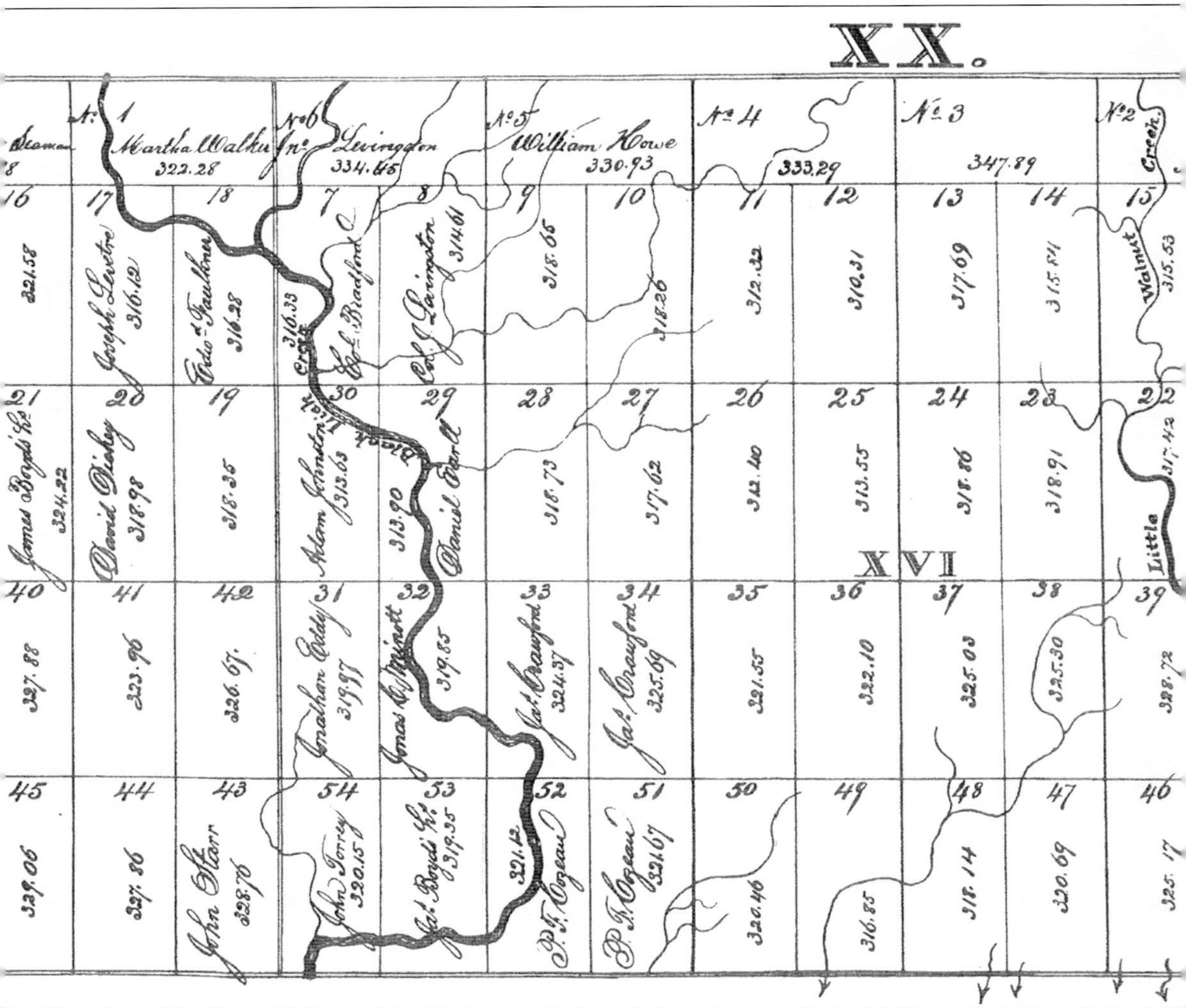

1801 Map of Refugee Tract Land. The Refugee Lands were established by the Continental Congress on April 13, 1785. The acreage was awarded to the refugees who fought for the Americans in the Revolutionary War. Many came from Scotland to escape persecution from the Catholics. Their ships landed in Truro, Nova Scotia—hence the name Truro Township. The tract is 4.5 miles wide and 48 miles long, covering a total of 58,080 acres through Franklin, Fairfield, Licking, and Perry Counties. Each section was approximately 320 acres, and they were awarded to soldiers or their widows and families. Many sold their land. In 1813, Daniel Dunihue bought 320 acres in Half Section 30W from the heirs of Revolutionary War soldier Adam Johnston for $600. In 1816, Dunihue bought 3.5 acres from Thomas Palmer. Late in 1816, Dunihue sold the 3.5 acres and most of Half Section 30W for $850 to John French, who had the land surveyed for a town. Reynoldsburg is located in Half Sections of 7 and 30 in Range 20 of the map. (Courtesy of Linda Bronstein.)

David Pugh (1768–1857). Truro Township was established in 1810. By 1816, it had 260 inhabitants. Pugh was among the first to arrive. He was a pioneer who traveled from Wales to Delaware County, then, in 1804, to Truro Township. Once he was in Truro Township, he built two toll bridges, owned a tavern, cleared a farm, and fathered seven children. (Courtesy of Eleanor Wilson Shonting.)

David Pugh Jr. and Hannah Phillips Pugh. David Pugh Jr. (1814–1877) first married Elizabeth Whitsel (1817–1857), and in 1861 he married Hannah Phillips (1817–1888). He fathered 10 children with Elizabeth, including David Franklin Pugh (1845–1928), who was appointed as a common pleas judge by Gov. Joseph B. Foraker in 1887. (Courtesy of Cornelia M. Parkinson.)

James and Mary Enlows. James (1825–1863) was orphaned, and he grew up in the family of David Taylor. When he was 22, he bought 307.25 acres of land from C. and M. Higgins on the west end of Truro Township, and the following year, he bought 40.35 acres from David Jones in the same area. In 1852, he married Mary A. Wolf (1827–1878). In 1854, he bought 30.23 acres from S. and C.A. Brush. In 1862, he bought 102 acres from Isaac Wolf in Columbus. When he was 37 years old, he enlisted to serve in the Civil War and became a first sergeant in Company D, 95th Regiment, of the Ohio Volunteer Infantry. James became ill while serving and died in the Regimental Hospital in Oak Ridge, Mississippi, at age 38. He was survived by his widow, Mary, and five children. (Courtesy of Cornelia M. Parkinson.)

EPHRAIM KUNKLE. Ephraim (1843–1915) was the son of Jacob Kunkle (1818–1909) and Susanna Loos (1821–1891). He was one of eight children and married Carrie Huff. Ephraim was raised in a home of strict and serious prayer. The parents wore only black clothing; the house had no mirrors, pictures, or musical instruments. Jacob was a minister in the River Brethren (later Brethren in Christ Church). (Courtesy of Jeanne Tenge Shook.)

BROTHERS THOMAS JEFFERSON AND TUNIS A. MCNAGHTEN. Pictured is an 1850s Ambrotype of Thomas Jefferson McNaghten (on the left, 1839–1911) and Tunis McNaghten (1846–1919). In 1868, Tunis was married to Martha "Mattie" Jane Pugh (1844–1930). They settled on McNaughten Road in Truro Township. Mattie was a relative of the famous Indian fighter, Lewis Wetzel, and granddaughter of justice of the peace Daniel Whetsel. (Courtesy of Eleanor Wilson Shonting.)

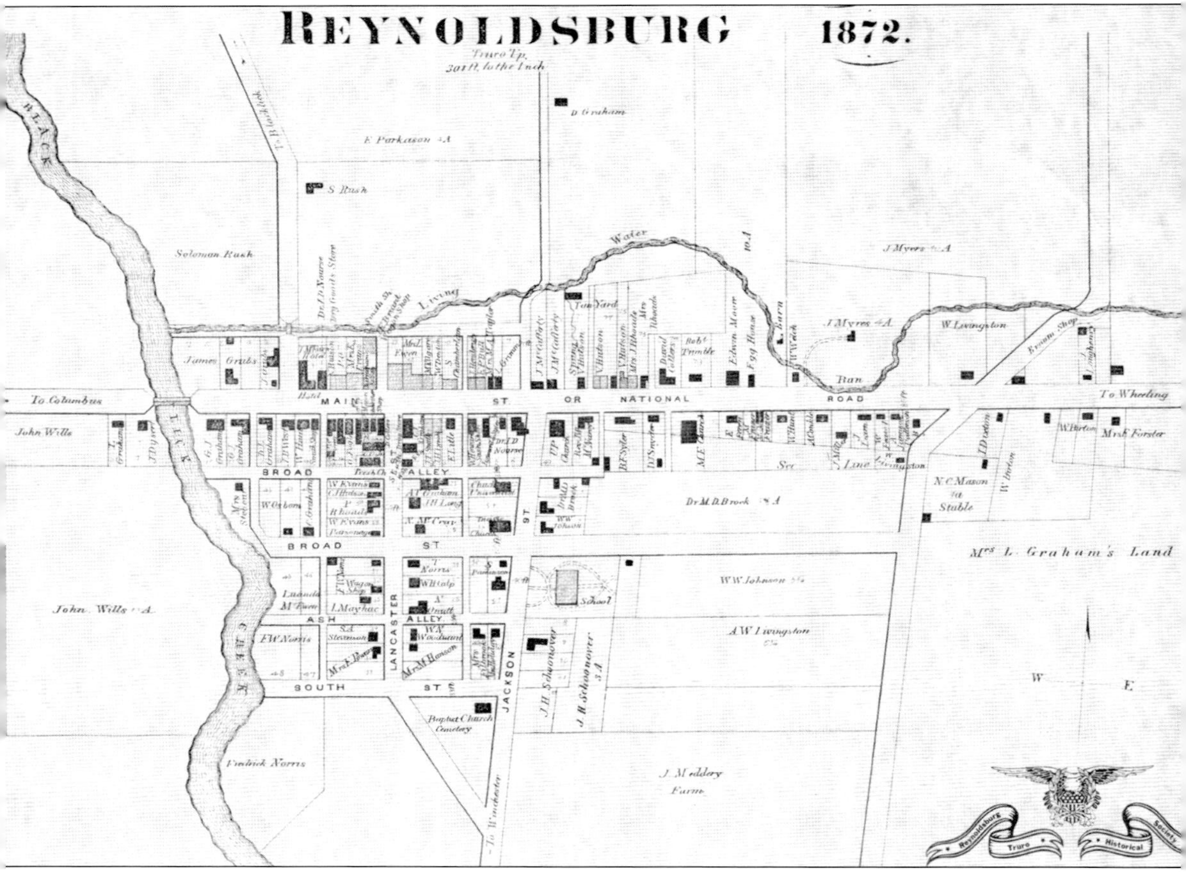

1872 Map of Reynoldsburg. This map notes property owners by name, and a separate attachment includes the "Reynoldsburgh Advertising Business Directory." Advertisers include "James Grubs, Dealer in Pianos, Organs, and Melodeons; William Evans, Blacksmith and Manufacturer of Spring Wagons and Buggies; J.W. McNary, Pastor of the United Presbyterian Church; A.W. Livingston and Son, Garden Seed growers; Dr. J.D. Nourse, Physician and Surgeon; Robert Trumble, Justice of the Peace; William Bowscher, Boot and Shoe Maker. Keeps on hand a choice lot of Boots and Shoes; V. Hutson, Dealer in Groceries and Provisions, and Postmaster; Jefferson Learn, Boot and Shoe Maker. All work done to order; and S.H. Lynch, Manufacturer of Monuments and Tombstones. Marble of the finest quality is used. All who wish to purchase will do well to call and examine before purchasing elsewhere." (Courtesy of RTHS.)

Joseph Bigelow Powell and Mary Selina Fancher. At the age of 30, Joseph Powell (1822–1913) came home from the California Gold Rush a wealthy man. In 1863, he married Lucinda French (1842–1870), and the couple had three children: Clement M. (1864–1926), William A. (1866–1890), and Andrew Jackson (1868–1955). Lucinda died in 1870. In 1876, Joseph married Selina Fancher (1852–1937), and they had three children: Gerda M. (Howell, 1878–1974), Flavia Elma (Valentine, 1883–1964), and Vashti Etheldine (Simms, 1888–1918). Joseph founded the town of Brice, arranged for the railroad to go through, established the Brice Clay Company, and built a grain elevator that remained in service for 77 years. Selina, his second wife, was the first female member of the Truro Township Board of Education and was an honorary member of the Columbus Chapter of the Daughters of the War of 1812. (Courtesy of Cornelia M. Parkinson.)

The Mound at Hibernia. In the heart of Hibernia was a large hill, and at the top was a mound built by prehistoric indigenous peoples. In August 1959, the mound was excavated. Inside the Davis mound (so named for the landowner), were bones of Archaic Period indigenous peoples under an Adena Period burial pit. Dr. Raymond S. Baby, archaeologist of the Ohio Historical Society, announced that there had been 27 burials in the Adena Period (800 BC to 700 AD), and under that were six Archaic skeletons from the period 6000 BC to 1500 BC. The bones were at least 3,000 years old. Dr. Baby explained that the Archaic man was long-headed and thin-faced. The six Archaic skeletons were huddled in a curved grave. The Adena skeletons had broad, flat faces and flattish heads. (Courtesy of Cornelia M. Parkinson.)

Two

Religious Freedom and Freedom from Slavery

Ben Patterson. Working for Alexander Livingston, the seed man, Ben Patterson (1836–1914) never fought in the Civil War but risked his life to help others. One of his duties was to transport runaway enslaved people in Livingston's covered wagon, which was called the Ark. Patterson would sometimes travel the entire night taking formerly enslaved people to Granville, Utica, or as far as Mount Vernon. (Courtesy of Cornelia M. Parkinson.)

THE SECEDER CHURCH (UNITED PRESBYTERIAN). The Seceder church was organized in 1816, and the group's first log church was built in 1817. In 1858, the Associate Presbyterian Church (Seceders) and the Associate Reformed Presbyterian Church (Covenanters) joined the United Presbyterian Church of North America. From then on, the Seceders were called United Presbyterians. After the original log church burned, a new church was built on Main Street in 1861. Due to a fire in 1916, a third structure (pictured above) was built. After a 1946 fire, another church (pictured below) was built in 1949. In November 2020, the 1949 building was sold and, after 203 years of existence, the congregation was disbanded. (Above, courtesy of Vernon B. McCall; below, courtesy of Mary Turner Stoots.)

PRIMITIVE BAPTIST CHURCH. The Primitive Baptist Church was first organized by elder John Hanover at John Coons's home in September 1822. It was called Friendship Church and Predestinarian Baptist Church. In the 1830s, a frame-and-brick structure was built. Around 1861, the church was demolished and rebuilt using 1,200 donated bricks leftover from the construction of pastor George N. Tusing's house. (Courtesy of Cornelia M. Parkinson.)

THE UNITED METHODIST CHURCH. The Methodist Episcopal church began as a bible class about 1835, meeting in a log schoolhouse. Around 1836, a frame structure was built on the southeast corner of Broad Street (now Broadwyn Drive) and Jackson Street. A brick building was erected on Main Street in 1871. After enrollment passed 2,000, the congregation moved to a new building on Graham Road in 1968. (Courtesy of RTHS.)

The First Presbyterian Church. This church was organized in 1836 and was built in 1840. The church burned down in 1861 and was rebuilt the same year. The congregation moved to a new site on Livingston Avenue and built a third church in 1963; it was called the Parkview Presbyterian Church. As of 2020, Parkview is now the Unity Presbyterian Church. (Courtesy of RTHS.)

Presbyterian Ladies Aid Society, 1915–1920. Members of the society pictured here include, from left to right: (first row) Dora Kitzmiller, Mrs. Forrester, Mary Jane Kenney, and Etta Johnson; (second row) Belle Carpenter, Phoebe Johnson, and Orpha Weeks; (third row) Lydia Oldham, Susan McIntyre, Cora Devore, Mrs. Manley, Edith Rush, Mrs. Welch, Ethel Johnson, and Mary McCray. (Courtesy of Margaret Ruvoldt.)

It Began as the Society of Powell's Chapel in Brice. In 1828, some of the area's new arrivals formed a society and began the construction of a church. A frame was completed, but then the most active and financially able members became sick and died; the framework eventually rotted. In 1850, another group was organized. In 1851, a church was erected. As the village of Brice grew, the congregation decided to replace the building and change the name to Brice Methodist Church. It later became Brice United Methodist Church. The Brice Ladies Aid Society paid for the carpets, chandeliers, and other equipment and made a pledge to help pay for the building. They held bake sales and quilt sales and served endless dinners cooked on a coal-burning cookstove in the small basement. The church was a center of entertainment, hosting revival meetings and socials as well as a series of Redpath Chautauqua lectures and musical programs that played to a packed house. (Courtesy of Cornelia M. Parkinson and Mary Turner Stoots.)

MESSIAH LUTHERAN CHURCH. In June 1958, pastor Donald Fritz met with 34 people in the basement of the Reynoldsburg First Presbyterian Church, and they decided to form a Lutheran congregation. By June 1959, a chapel had been dedicated. In April 1968, a new church sanctuary was dedicated. (Courtesy of Cornelia M. Parkinson.)

CHURCH OF CHRIST. This church had three different names: Church of Christ, Disciples, and Campbellite. All three referred to Alexander Campbell, who was born in Ireland in 1788 and came to the United States in 1809. He was not an ordained clergyman but created his own variety of Protestantism called the Disciples of Christ. The congregation was organized in 1863, and the church was constructed in 1870. (Courtesy of Mary Turner Stoots.)

MACEDONIAN ORTHODOX CATHEDRAL OF THE DORMITION OF THE VIRGIN MARY. Founded in 1958, this church, also known as St. Mary, is a Macedonian Orthodox church located in Reynoldsburg. It is one of the oldest Macedonian Orthodox communities in the United States and American/Canadian Diocese. The congregation's first church was built in Whitehall, where they worshipped for over 40 years. In 2003, the parish community purchased a 14-acre property in Reynoldsburg, and a new church was built on Waggoner Road and dedicated on October 22, 2006. The "Dormition of the Most Holy Birth-giver of God" fresco (pictured below) on the western wall of the cathedral was completed in 2010 and donated by the Macedonian Orthodox Philanthropic Society of Columbus. (Both, courtesy of Mary Turner Stoots.)

St. Pius X Catholic Church. On September 6, 1958, seventy-five members of the new parish met at the home of Joseph Herbert. The St. Pius X community first gathered around the Altar of Christ at French Run School on September 21, 1958. Ground was broken for a new parish in August 1959, and the final church building was dedicated in October 1969. (Courtesy of Mary Turner Stoots.)

Williams Noe. Williams Noe (1817–1869) was born in Plain Township. In 1842, he married Isabella Pugh (1820–1850), daughter of David Pugh. They had six sons; three died in infancy. Two years after Isabella died, Williams married Permelia Hanson (1810–1869). Williams was a strong advocate of abolition and doubtlessly worked for the Underground Railroad. (Courtesy of Cornelia M. Parkinson.)

David and Nancy Graham. When he was 16, David Graham (1801–1886) moved with his family to Ohio. At 18, he was employed as a schoolteacher in a log schoolhouse on his father's farm. In 1821, David married Nancy Graham (1803–1889). They had 10 children: Matilda Dickey (Livingston, 1823–1883), Maria (1824–1843), Samuel, James McLean (1828–1914), William Beveridge (1829–1896), Sarah Jane (Johnson, 1832–1913), David Lindsay (1835–1911), Margaret D. (Lunn, 1837–1915), George McBurney, and Anna Mary (McCrory, 1844–1922). Men risked heavy fines, jail, and even their lives by harboring runaway enslaved people. Their houses served as stations and havens of safety for those attempting to reach freedom. David Graham was a devoted abolitionist and a faithful Presbyterian. Nancy Graham bore five sons and five daughters. Her eldest, Matilda Dickey, married Alexander W. Livingston, whose covered wagon was used to transport enslaved people to freedom. (Courtesy of Cornelia M. Parkinson.)

David Graham House. The David Graham house at 1812 Epworth Avenue was built around 1858. It famously served as an Underground Railroad station. Sometimes called the Hillhouse House, for 25 years, it was the home of Charlotte and Albert S. Hillhouse, both of whom died in 1954. Many descendants of the Grahams lived and worked diligently for their church and community in Reynoldsburg. (Courtesy of Cornelia M. Parkinson.)

The Ark (Replica). Alexander Livingston used his wagon with seats on the sides to transport his large family to Sunday church services. Such an important citizen could not transport fugitives overnight, as his absence would be noticed. His employee, Ben Patterson, took on the task, which could cost him huge fines, his home, or his life. This replica was built by Arthur Phalor. (Courtesy of Mary Turner Stoots.)

Three

FAMILIES AND HOMES

RODEBAUGH COUSINS (1900). Harry (1896–1962) and (Karl) Dana Rodebaugh (1896–1988) are shown sitting on J.A. Pettit's doorstep on Broad Street in 1900. Broad Street was later renamed Broadwyn Drive so it would not be confused with Route 16, which was also called Broad Street. (Courtesy of K.D. Rodebaugh.)

The Lincoln D. Black Family. Lincoln Black (1868–1948) graduated from Reynoldsburg Union Academy in 1892. He owned his farm and was a Columbus mail carrier. In 1924, he married Mary Josephine (Herndon) Hawks (1886–1957). Lincoln had two brothers, Edward (born in 1861) and Clarence R. (1865–1933), and one sister, Carrie (1874–1907). Clarence graduated from Reynoldsburg Union Academy in 1890, and Carrie graduated in 1896. (Courtesy of Cornelia M. Parkinson.)

The Henry Phalor Family. Henry and Rebecca Phalor were married in 1875 and had 11 children. From left to right are (first row, seated) Viola (Hickerson, 1884–1982), Henry (1847–1915), Chester Hare (1895–1978), Rebecca (1858–1938), and Iva Belle (1887–1975); (second row, standing) Elizabeth Maud (Johnson, 1881–1966), David Clinton (1883–1956), Kathryn (Wolf, 1876–1968), Arthur (1890–1990), Della Estella (Hellems, 1880–1973), William Henry (1877–1947), Anna May (1886–1949), and Samuel (1878–1921). (Courtesy of Cornelia M. Parkinson.)

Josiah R. and Margaret Graham Lunn. In 1833, Josiah Lunn's parents were traveling through Reynoldsburg and stopped overnight. When they were leaving, a tug broke on their horse's harness. They stayed to fix it. After watching the sun rise on the beauty of the Ohio valley, they decided to stay. Josiah Lunn (1831–1923) and Margaret Graham (1838–1915) married in 1856. Margaret was a daughter of David and Nancy Graham. Josiah served for many years on the Reynoldsburg Board of Education. The couple had seven children, including Estella M. "Esta" (1866–1952), David Josiah (1874–1922), Dewit Birney (1875–1965), and twin daughters Izora Nancy (1859–1934) and Eldora Elizabeth (Graham, 1859–1947). Izora did not marry but instead lived at home and tended to her parents' needs through their illnesses and deaths. Eldora married Leonard Graham, registrar of Muskingum College. (Courtesy of Cornelia M. Parkinson.)

Joseph Thomas Ashton and Hannah Catharine Vernon. Joseph Ashton (1831–1904) and Hannah Vernon (1836–1906) married in 1859. They had five sons and three daughters. Joseph was a farmer, and he had a large brick house on the current site of Stoney Creek Country Club. In 1861, Joseph bought the first reaper ever seen in this area. (Courtesy of Martha Ashton Brown.)

William Vernon Ashton Sr. and Birdie Alice Green. William Ashton (1860–1917) married Laura Woodruff, who died at the age of 29 in 1893. They had one child. Birdie Green (1869–1945) graduated from Reynoldsburg Union Academy in 1892. She taught school for nine years, then married William in 1901. Eleven months later, they had twins Hannah and Joseph. William "Pete" was born in 1909. (Courtesy of Martha Ashton Brown.)

Hannah Jane Ashton, Joseph Covert "Joe" Ashton, and William Vernon "Pete" Ashton Jr. In 1920, Hannah Ashton (1901–2000, seated on the left) graduated from Reynoldsburg High School, and four years later she received her bachelor's degree from Ohio State University. For two years, she taught at Scotia, a Presbyterian boarding school in North Carolina. She was hired by the Reynoldsburg Board of Education in May 1928 and spent the next 34 years as a teacher, confidante, job counselor, and administrator. Joseph Ashton (1901–1983, standing) was a farmer. His former farmland is now Blacklick Woods Metropolitan Park and Unity Presbyterian Church. William Vernon "Pete" (1909–1988, seated on the right) became a farmer and was a longtime member of the Jasper Lodge of the Knights of Pythias. He was a York Rite Mason and Scottish Rite Mason and has been awarded the York Cross of Honor. The Scottish Rite awarded him the 33rd Degree—the highest honor in Masonry. (Courtesy of Cornelia M. Parkinson.)

William Vernon "Pete" Ashton Jr. Pete (1909–1988) was a 1927 graduate of Reynoldsburg High School. As a farmer, he knew his land and its capabilities, and he used this knowledge to his advantage. He was Past Master of Reynoldsburg Lodge 340, Free and Accepted Masons, and was a 33rd-Degree Mason. (Courtesy of Martha Ashton Brown and RTHS.)

George Nelson Tusing and Elizabeth Harman. Elizabeth (1829–1914) was the daughter of Thomas Harman (1785–1848) and Elizabeth Rarey (1787–1870). She married George Tusing (1821–1905) at the age of 18, and they had nine children. George was an accomplished farmer and a Baptist minister for 30 years. His work is mentioned in a half-dozen histories of various counties. (Courtesy of Laura Tussing McClarren and Margaret Ruvoldt.)

Four Generations of the Myers Family. This c. 1900 photograph includes, from left to right, (first row) Edythe Myers (1881–1961) and her great-grandmother Lucinda Search Rochelle (1809–1903); (second row) Edythe's mother, Mary Elizabeth Hickman Myers (1857–1957), and grandmother Mary Ann Rochelle Hickman (1837–1941). (Courtesy of Wayne Myers.)

The George N. Tusing Family. Pictured here are, from left to right, (first row) Louisa Rhoads (1847–1934), Leroy Whitcomb (1848–1931), Elizabeth Harman (1829–1914), Laura Elva (Donaldson, 1860–1943), George N. Tusing (1821–1905), and Lewis Benton (1858–1930); (second row) Sarah Jane (White, 1852–1932), Silas Fristoe White (1842–1930), Margaret Elizabeth (McNaughten, 1861–1938), Huldah Rhoads (Tussing, 1852–1933), Clinton Wiley (1849–1940), Dr. Frank G. Taylor (1851–1905), and Mary Ellen (Taylor, 1854–1947). (Courtesy of Sylvia Tussing Hering.)

Roger, Russell, Homer, and Fred Tussing. The brothers were sons of Llewellyn W. "Len" Tussing and Cora Palmer. Roger (1913–2006) was a farmer near Fredericktown. Russell (1907–1988) graduated from Ohio State University and was a plant engineer for National Cash Register. Homer (1897–1965) owned a Shell gas station. Fred (1895–1978) was a farmer and state sheep-shearing champion before electric shears were in widespread use. (Courtesy of Whit Tussing.)

Four Generations of the Hickman Family. This photograph was taken around 1900. The Hickman ladies are, from left to right, (first row) Anna Wolf Johnson Shaulis and her great-grandmother Lucinda Search Rochelle (1809–1903); (second row) Anna's mother, Josephine Hickman Wolf (1881–1961), and grandmother Mary Ann Rochelle Hickman (1837–1941). (Courtesy of Wayne Myers.)

ALEXANDER W. LIVINGSTON FAMILY. Alexander W. Livingston (1821–1898) and Matilda Dickey Graham (1823–1883) married in 1844 and had 10 children. The eldest, John, died at age two. Their family members pictured here are, from left to right, (first row) John "Judd" (1861–1948), Martha (1863–1934), and Josiah (1859–1943); (second row) Nancy (1851–1938), Matilda, Alexander, Robert (1849–1940), and Mary (1857–1929); (third row) Samuel (1855–1899), David (1847–1924), and William (1853–1898). (Courtesy of Linda Bronstein.)

ROBERT AND NETTIE LIVINGSTON. Robert Livingston (1849–1940) was the third son of Alexander W. Livingston, the man who cultivated the first commercial tomato. Robert married Nettie Forrester (1852–1928) in 1872. Robert was president of the Livingston Seed Company in Columbus, Ohio, after his father moved to Des Moines, Iowa, in 1880. (Courtesy of Linda Bronstein.)

The William Wells Johnson Family. This c. 1880 photograph features the William Wells Johnson family. In 1876, W.W. Johnson represented the entire grammar department of Reynoldsburg Union Academy. Pictured here are, from left to right, (seated) Sarah Jane Graham Johnson, Jennie Johnson, and William Wells Johnson; (seated on the arm of the chair) Jesse Johnson; (standing) William S. Johnson, Anna Johnson, Fayette Johnson, and Mary Johnson. (Courtesy of Linda Bronstein.)

The Taylor Family Double. The structure on the right served as home to Mary Tusing (wife of Dr. Frank G. Taylor) and her daughter Zella and son Frank. Later, Frank's sister Georgia T. Headley lived in the south (left) side, and her sister Zella lived on the north side. Once Taylor's barn, it was moved south across an alley to this site, and David Foltz, carpenter-contractor, converted it into a family dwelling. (Courtesy of Cornelia M. Parkinson.)

MARTHA JANE PUGH AND TUNIS A. MCNAGHTEN. Martha Jane Pugh (1844–1932) was called Mattie or Jennie, and she married Tunis McNaghten (1846–1919) in 1868. They settled in a large home on McNaughten Road (pictured below) and had two children, Estella Blanch "Stella" (1869–1957) and Stewart Alexander (1876–1962). Tunis was very active in the GAR (Grand Army of the Republic) and pushed his wife into joining the Women's Relief Corps. They also belonged to the Grange and to the church. They participated in the Decoration Day ceremonies in Mason Hall and Silent Home Cemetery. In 1876, Tunis became Worshipful Master of Reynoldsburg Lodge No. 340, F&A (Free and Accepted) Masons. He also served as Worshipful Master in 1877, 1878, 1879, 1886, 1887, 1890, 1894, and 1912. (Both, courtesy of Eleanor Wilson Shonting.)

Thomas Jefferson McNaghten. This picture from the mid-1860s is a tintype positive image (painted on iron) of Thomas Jefferson McNaghten (1839–1911), the son of Thomas McNaghten (1787–1863) and Mary Stover Grove (1801–1866). Thomas Jefferson McNaghten was married three times—in 1861, to Lucretia F. Bull (1844–1864); in 1866, to Barbara A. Deeds (1840–1870); and in 1874, to Alma Francina Ashbrook (1848–1924). (Courtesy of Eleanor Wilson Shonting.)

Five Generations of the McNaghten Family, 1965. This photograph includes five generations of the McNaghten family. Pictured here are Blanche Holcomb McNaghten, who is seated and holding her great-great-granddaughter, Myla Elaine Schumers; standing are Carol Shonting Schumers (left) and her mother, Eleanor Wilson Shonting (center), and Eleanor's mother, Lola McNaghten Wright (daughter of Blanche). (Courtesy of Eleanor Wilson Shonting.)

Five Generations of the McNaghten Family, 1992. This photograph also includes five generations of the McNaghten family. Myla Schumers Outlaw is seated on the left and holding her son, Matthew Slone Outlaw, and Myla's great-grandmother Lola McNaghten Wright is seated on the right. Standing are Myla's mother, Carol Shonting Schumers (left), and Carol's mother (and Lola's daughter), Eleanor Wilson Shonting. (Courtesy of Eleanor Wilson Shonting.)

John H. Motz Residence, 1916. In 1891, John H. Motz (1865–1956) married Martha Beery (1866–1964). John bought the grain elevator from Joseph Powell in 1893. John was president of Ohio Federal Savings and Loan Association for about 50 years. After Martha's death, their house was converted into the Brice Post Office, which remained in use until 1989, when the new post office was dedicated. (Courtesy of Dorothy Motz Evans.)

THE MORRISON FAMILY IN 1900. On Waggoner Road stands the Morrison Homestead. The family included, from left to right, Samuel, Eliza, William, Isabelle, John, and William (younger). John, the elder William's father, was a stonemason who came to the United States in 1849. In 1861, he occupied the homestead, building the house later. The brick was made in Taylor Station, and the stone was quarried from Blacklick Creek. (Courtesy of Mary P. Morrison.)

THE FRANK G. TAYLOR HOUSE. This was once the home of Dr. John Nourse. In 1877, Nourse sold it to Dr. Frank G. Taylor, physician and surgeon. Until about 1952, when Jane (Connell) Taylor died, it was the home of this prominent family. Harold "Pick" Richardson, antiques dealer, lived here for over 25 years. The house was sold to Ralph and Dorothy Tate in 1980. (Courtesy of Cornelia M. Parkinson.)

Gilbert and Susannah Taylor Green. In 1831, Gilbert Green (1804–1878) came to Ohio with his wife, Mary Belinda Harrison (1809–1833). They married in 1826 and had three children. Gilbert bought 318 acres in two separate purchases. Mary Belinda passed away at the age of 26. In 1834, Gilbert married Susannah Taylor (1808–1886). In 1835, Gilbert bought an additional 118 acres. (Courtesy of Cornelia M. Parkinson.)

John Wolf. In 1831, Jacob Wolf Sr. and Margaret Cornell Wolf moved to Truro Township along with their five children (they would eventually have five more). At that time, the oldest son, John, was 15 years old. In 1837, John (1815–1889) married Ann Cornell (1829–1900); they had three children and owned 143 acres in Truro Township and a small farm in Licking County. (Courtesy of Cornelia M. Parkinson.)

The Oldham Farm, 1898. James A. Oldham (1842–1933) taught school for a short time after he graduated from high school, then enlisted as a Union soldier in 1862 and served as a member of Company K, 133rd Regiment, Ohio Volunteer Infantry. His regiment was sent to destroy the Richmond & Petersburg Railway, one of the means by which the Confederates received their supplies. The Rebels put up a hot battle. James was given a medical discharge, and in 1864, he married Laura G. Hart (1844–1925). They moved to Waggoner Road, and the house is still on that property today. Members of the Oldham family pictured here are (seated) Laura Hart Oldham and James Oldham; (standing, from left to right) Mary (married John Morrison), Harriet (married James McOwen), Zola (married Robert Barb), Nannie Tussing Oldham (behind James), Collins (Nannie's husband), Cyril, and Morton. (Courtesy of Clark Oldham.)

The Connell (Connal, Connel) Family. The children of Rachel Elsey (1827–1896, granddaughter of John D. and Jane Graham French) and James Connel (1824–1903, son of James and Helen Connal) are gathered here. Rachel and James had eight children, but only seven lived to adulthood. Flora Bell died at the age of three (1859–1863). James was a United Presbyterian deacon. From left to right are (first row) Helen Elizabeth (1850–1921, married Palmer Henderson) and Ada (1870–1947, married Will Smith in 1890); (second row) Albert (1857–1908), Andrew (1854–1944), and John (1853–1928); (third row) David Potter (1860–1940) and James McNary (1865–1909). In 1884, Albert married Ella Sarah White (1864–1947). Albert and Ella are the parents of Elzy Connell (1885–1948) and the grandparents of Ralph Lynn Connell (1925–2007). Ralph married Jean Hamilton (1924–2016), from Brice, and they have two daughters: Charity and Sarah. This photograph was probably taken in the mid-1880s. (Courtesy of Ralph Connell.)

One of Reynoldsburg's First Housing Developments. Brookside Park was the first modular housing development in Reynoldsburg. In 1955, the zoning commission was established, and National Homes broke ground to build 714 homes for Brookside Park in 1956. Between 1950 and 1960, the area population increased by over 976 percent due to the influx of people working at Western Electric, the Defense Construction and Supply Center, North American Aviation, Timken Roller Bearing Company, and Lockbourne Airforce Base. By 1962, Reynoldsburg had gone from housing all grades in one school building to having four elementary schools and a new high school. Brookside Park homes were well-built one-story modular homes constructed on concrete slabs and comfortable for families. The prices ranged between \$11,000 and \$12,000. With a down payment of \$350, the house payments were \$79 per month. (Both, courtesy of Ken Sperry.)

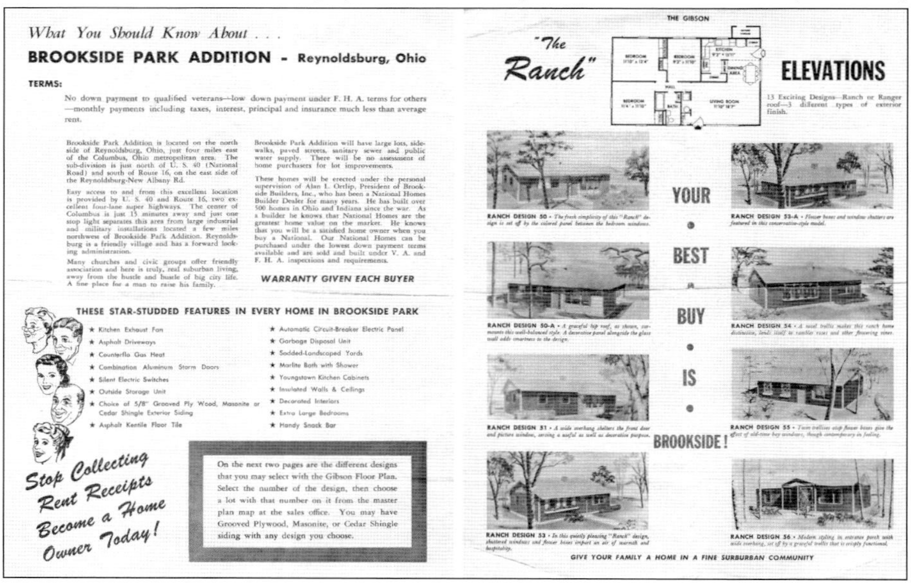

Four

SCHOOLS

REYNOLDSBURG UNION ACADEMY, 1917. A large two-story building was built at Jackson Street and Broadwyn Drive in 1868. The Reynoldsburg Union Academy was the first public high school in Franklin County. Dr. Darlington J. Snyder was the first superintendent and high school teacher. Other instructors taught the lower grades. (Courtesy of RTHS.)

DR. DARLINGTON JOSEPH SNYDER. Darlington J. Snyder (1843–1917) was the most remarkable man to ever come into the Reynoldsburg schools. He organized the schools, expanded them, and kept them running at top speed for 28 years. He went to school in New Salem and to the Union Academy in Fairfield County. In 1868, he graduated from Ohio Wesleyan University with a bachelor of arts degree. In 1869, he began his career in Reynoldsburg, and that same year, he married Lomira F. Landon. Darlington attained his master's degree in 1871 from Ohio Wesleyan University. Students enrolled at Reynoldsburg from all around Ohio—and some from outside the state—based on Dr. Snyder's reputation and credentials. Dr. Snyder was a 32nd Degree Mason, Master of the Reynoldsburg Masonic Lodge in 1883, a member of the Odd Fellows and Eastern Star, and charter member of the Jasper Lodge of the Knights of Pythias. He belonged to the National Medical Association and the Ohio State Medical Association. (Courtesy of Cornelia M. Parkinson.)

NOTEWORTHY SUPERINTENDENTS. From 1868 to 1981, Reynoldsburg has had 22 school superintendents. Most stayed up to three years. However, Dr. Darlington J. Snyder and the three men pictured here served Reynoldsburg Schools for a total of 74 years. James A. Oppy (right) was superintendent for 15 years, from 1929 to 1944; Clifford R. Mobberly (at left in the below image) was superintendent for 14 years, from 1944 to 1958; and Robert P. Heischman came to Reynoldsburg in 1958 and retired in 1974 after serving 16 years. (Right, courtesy of RTHS; below courtesy of Cornelia M. Parkinson.)

THE CLASS OF 1899. This photograph is the oldest class picture in the Reynoldsburg-Truro Historical Society Museum collection. When the students were moved to the new Livingston Avenue High School in 1962, the class composites and photographs were removed from the walls, where they had graced the halls for 63 years. All the pictures were stored in a closet off the third-floor study hall and were not discovered again until 1973, when Jim Kielmeyer found them by accident while doing custodial work. Kielmeyer told Jack Kitzmiller, who was president of the Reynoldsburg High School Alumni Association at the time. Shirley Tudor Vingle and Rollie Powell happened to be present when Kitzmiller heard the news, so the three of them confiscated the photographs for the Reynoldsburg-Truro Historical Society with the permission of principal Michael Zorich. In this photograph are, from left to right, (seated) Grace D. Bowen-Belt, unidentified teacher, and Ione M. Bunn; (standing) Georgia Taylor Headley, Claude Melnott Osborne, William O. Winegarner, Frank Graham, and Olive Medbery. (Courtesy of RTHS.)

1906 Reynoldsburg Upper Classmen. Grades 9 through 12 are pictured outside the Reynoldsburg School with the class of 1906 seniors in the front rows. The school building housed all grades. Superintendent Arthur L. Gantz (1877–1956) is at farthest left in the fourth row. The Reynoldsburg Union Academy was built in 1868. The name was changed to Reynoldsburg School sometime between 1900 and 1916. (Courtesy of Cornelia M. Parkinson.)

1920 Elementary School Photograph. Ettie Louise Waid (1890–1963) gathered her elementary students outside of the Reynoldsburg School for a class picture in 1920. The following year, she married Floyd Johnson Vance (1893–1975). Floyd and Ettie moved to Westerville, Ohio, shortly thereafter, when he became the registrar and dean of Otterbein College. (Courtesy of RTHS.)

VERENNA PALMER. Verenna Palmer (1902–1971) graduated from Glenford High School in Glenford, Ohio, and later from Kent State University, where she was the May queen. She also starred in a Cleveland production of *No, No, Nanette*. She began teaching in Licking County, where, due to the shortage of men during the war, she coached football and taught shop. The county voted her Teacher of the Year in 1940. In 1942, she began her junior high school career in Reynoldsburg. She has been an advisor for the dramatics, science, art, and English clubs; she also coached the debate team and junior high cheerleaders and served as a senior advisor. Until 1971, she never missed a day of school. She was totally dedicated to giving her students the human aspect of history. (Courtesy of RTHS.)

HIBERNIA SCHOOL CHILDREN. This photograph was taken in 1920 or 1921. This was the school's last full year in Truro Township. Starting in January 1923, Hibernia School pupils rode the Ohio Electric Railway (interurban train) to Reynoldsburg. In June 1926, the old Hibernia School and grounds were sold to William Cook in Brice for $4,425. (Courtesy of Paul Moore.)

REYNOLDSBURG SCHOOL, 1926. On November 24, 1924, an election was held for locals to vote on $100,000 in bonds to add on to the existing school's brick building. The 1924 school year cost $31,213 in total operation and maintenance, including the superintendent's salary of $1,500. In 1925, rooms were added to the outside perimeter of the two-story brick Reynoldsburg School structure, along with a third floor. (Courtesy of RTHS.)

SECOND-GRADE CLASS AT BRICE ELEMENTARY SCHOOL, 1928. The Village of Brice had a two-room elementary school that was situated on Brice Road facing Tussing Road on land that had been donated by George N. Tusing. Students went to Reynoldsburg for upper grade and high school classes. One of the students in this picture, Dorothy Motz Evans, celebrated her 100th birthday on January 1, 2021. From left to right are (first row) Betty Bulen, John Gibson, unidentified, ? Taylor, Maxine Zwayer, unidentified, Marjorie Stevenson, Jean Peters, Dorothy Motz, Jean Davis, Neil Stevenson, and Esther Petty; (second row) Mildred Lewis, Willard Rhodes, unidentified, Ruth Sawyer, Robert Dorsey, Leo Lamb, Theodore Grube, Paul Miller, Wilbur Baker, Betty Crist, Madge Kallies, and teacher Naomi Rawn. (Courtesy of Dorothy Motz Evans.)

1928 Girls' Basketball Team. This picture of the 1928 girls' basketball team has been identified by visual comparison with the 1928, 1929, 1930, and 1931 senior photographs of the girls in the picture. From left to right are (first row) Clara Pursley, Martha Graham, and unidentified; (second row) Mary Millar, Enid Joseph, unidentified, Irene Mays, and Thelma Gorman; (third row) unidentified, Edith Evans, and Dorothy Henderson. (Courtesy of RTHS.)

Reynoldsburg School, 1942. In 1941, classrooms, laboratories, mechanical drawing and industrial arts rooms, a gymnasium, and an equipped auditorium were added to the schoolhouse. The school board also rescinded its action taken in 1933 to not hire married women. Male teachers were getting drafted into World War II, and at last, female teachers had a semblance of equal employment opportunity. (Courtesy of RTHS.)

First-Grade Class of Ethel Berry, 1931. Ethel Berry taught school—usually first grade—for her entire adult life. During the Great Depression, at the December 1931 school board meeting, Berry attended with Helen Parkinson, four other teachers, the high school principal, and the superintendent. The six teachers representing the school decided to teach through December 24 on a half salary. (Courtesy of RTHS.)

Perley C. Milnor, Superintendent, 1920s. Perley C. "Pappy" Milnor (1887–1939) was superintendent from 1926 to 1929, then taught high school into the late 1930s. Teaching during the Great Depression meant that there were months on end when the teachers agreed to work for half of their salary. Milnor was greatly respected for his fairness and sense of the ridiculous. Dave McCoy, a high school student, asked classmate Keith Knox to prepare his theme. Knox gave McCoy no time to look at it before he had to read it aloud to the class. The last sentence was, "And this is why all old people die young." McCoy, aghast, turned red, and the class and Milnor nearly fell off their tablet-arm chairs laughing. When Milnor died in 1939, the board of education spread a Resolution of Respect upon the minutes. (Photograph by James Ruvoldt; courtesy of Cornelia M. Parkinson.)

Lillian "Margueriete" Click. Margueriete Click (1909–1984) was born in Reynoldsburg and graduated from Reynoldsburg High School in 1927. She went on to Bliss College and The Ohio State University, earning her bachelor of arts degree from Capital University. When she graduated in 1931, there were few teaching jobs available. She began teaching in Reynoldsburg in 1942, combining her interests in languages and journalism. Margueriete has taught English II, III, IV, French, Latin, public speaking, and business English. She was always involved in extracurricular activities. She was the advisor for the *Reynolian* yearbook from 1943 to 1963; advisor to Y-Teens, the French Club, and the Junior Classical League; and advisor for the senior play for 17 years. After 26 years of teaching, she retired in 1968, although she returned the following year and taught half days for five more years. (Courtesy of RTHS.)

REYNOLDSBURG'S FIRST YEARBOOK, 1943. The first *Reynolian* for Reynoldsburg High School was published in 1943. From left to right are (first row) June Stillwell Weber, Marie Butts Wagner, Sue McCray Miles, and Donna Turner Gordon; (second row, standing), Bill Nirote, Charles Hanners, assistant editor Mary Jane Tudor Schmidt, editor Connie McNary Parkinson, Leon Walker, and faculty advisor Margueriete Click. (Photograph by Herb Topolosky; courtesy of Cornelia M. Parkinson.)

AN INTERESTING DAY AT SCHOOL, 1917. This photograph appears to have been taken on either "show and tell" or "bring your chicken to school" day. Nine chickens are being held by young men in the front row, and what is possibly a taxidermized chicken rests atop the hat of the woman at far right in the front row. (Courtesy of Hannah J. Ashton.)

REYNOLDSBURG SIXTH-GRADE CLASS, 1937. Students do not always love their teachers, even good ones. Ralph Connell wrote next to his teacher's name, "The teacher with a piece of inner-tube to smack you with!" Pictured here are, from left to right, (first row) ? Wharton, Junior Osborne, unidentified, Wilford Carr, Dwight "Spike" Myers, Ben Weber, Budd Oldham, Alden "Pod" Hayes, and Bill Fischer; (second row) Marjorie Kielmeyer, Betty Bell Joseph, Patty Click, Mary Alice Karnes, Lagatha Walz, Mary Louise Shultis, Jane Kelsey, and Sybil Duffy; (third row) Doris Sanders, Grace King, unidentified, Janet Williams, unidentified, Mae Mitchell, Sue McCray, Jane Weaver, Vivian Montgomery, Birdella Butts, and teacher Samuel Raver; (fourth row) Jerry Nesser, Bill Brennon, Bill McCall, Jim Morris, Dick Krause, George Hastilow, Ralph Connell, Ray Kennedy, unidentified, ? Wharton, and Jim Little. (Courtesy of Charity and Ralph Connell.)

HANNAH JANE ASHTON, PRINCIPAL. Hannah Jane Ashton (1901–2000) graduated from Reynoldsburg High School in 1920, returning as a teacher in 1928. For the next 34 years, she served as a teacher and administrator. In August 1944, Ashton was appointed principal of the school. From then until she resigned in 1962, she served in an administrative capacity. When she decided the school needed a library, she visited every library in Franklin County to ask if they had any duplicate books to donate. The result of her efforts was a school library so popular that it was opened to the public. The former high school is now a middle school named in her honor—the Hannah J. Ashton School. A memorial stone (below), designed by Richard W. Parkinson, was dedicated on November 14, 1982, with Ashton in attendance. (Both, courtesy of RTHS.)

Truro Township School No. 3 and 1910 Elementary Students. An addition gave this Brice Road country school, built as a one-room structure, two rooms. It faced the end of Tussing Road. Teacher Bert Wildermuth stands at left; from left to right are (first row) Clara Bair, Ardella Tussing, Vinnie McClure, Mabel Bair, Elmer Bair, and Lawrence Wolf; (second row) ? Mason, Laura Tussing, Lena Chilcote, Viola Wolf, Ethel Mason, and Lucille McClure; (third row) Helen Tobin, Homer Tussing, Theodore McClure, Rhoda Chilcote, Rexford Rhodes, Raymond Bechtel, and Edith Motz; (fourth row) Byron McClure, Lloyd Motz, Elbert Burnett, Rolland Burnett, Lennie Chilcote, Clarence Fancher, Andrew Donovan, Carlton Burnett, and Guy McClure. (Above, courtesy of Cornelia M. Parkinson; below, photograph by Vernon W. Miller and courtesy of Laura McClarren and Edith Hummell.)

First-Grade Class at French Run Elementary School, 1959. Brookside Park was a huge modular housing development in Reynoldsburg. French Run was the first elementary school and was located next to Brookside Park. It was built in 1958 and opened in the fall to three of the six first-grade classes in town. Two were still held at the Methodist Episcopal church, and one class was at the Grange Hall. From left to right are (first row) Ray Whittle, Shirley Mossburg, Gail Purdum, Bobby Snow, Mary Turner, Jimmy Butts, Vickie Stewart, Butch Turner, Debra Metzler and Cindy Ballou; (second row) John Simpson, David Curnell, Tommy Dowdy, Sandra Cooke, Deborah Lamon, Steven Will, John Stockwell, Marc Grimm, Walter Schlosser, Terrie Renwick, and teacher Martha Savage; (third row) Jeannette Fouts, Debra Dellinger, Peter Jagodzinski, Mike Sayre, Sheila Herold, Mike Millar, Donnie Jeffrey, Randy Hughes, Becky Frazer, and Janis Hughes. (Courtesy of RTHS.)

MARTHA GRAHAM SAVAGE. Martha Graham Savage (1910–2007) graduated from Reynoldsburg High School in 1928 and received a two-year teaching certificate from Muskingum College in New Concord, Ohio. She also attended Berea College and The Ohio State University. She began her teaching career in Obetz, Ohio, where she met and married Elton D. Savage (1903–1987) in 1941. She taught first grade in Reynoldsburg schools for more than 20 years. She was known for her patience with her first-graders, her sunny personality, and her good humor. Her ties to the United Presbyterian Church of Reynoldsburg go back four generations, and her ancestors are buried in the historic Seceder Cemetery near Route 256. At age 13, Martha began playing piano for church services, and she continued to play piano (and later organ) until she was in her seventies. She became the first woman of that congregation to be ordained as an elder. She was a founding member of the Reynoldsburg-Truro Historical Society and spent thousands of hours helping to make the society's museum what it is today. (Courtesy of RTHS.)

Reynoldsburg Seventh and Eighth Grades, 1916. Lena "Linnie" Sprague, who was from a prominent local family, graduated from Reynoldsburg in 1908, went to college, and came back to teach. In a 1980 interview, she said that she and her husband, Pat Doherty, had spent 23 summers camping at Glacier National Park. Pictured here are her seventh- and eighth-grade students, including a young Hannah Ashton. From left to right are (first row) Archie Graham, Leon Morehead, Thomas Swope, Dale Graham, unidentified, and unidentified; (second row) Malcolm Fitzgerald, Bryant "Mickey" Slack, Carl Minor, Hugh Slack, ? Meharry, ? Krumm, and Wendell Fishpaw; (third row) Joe Ashton, Herbert Orem, Arthur Van Schoyck, Hannah Ashton, Alice Swope, Pearl Lucas, Mary Graham, and Sprague; (fourth row) Eunice Evans, unidentified, Florence Newman, Mary Fishpaw, Margaret Connell, Minerva Evans, and Lillian Warner. (Courtesy of Hannah J. Ashton.)

Reynoldsburg High School Marching Band, 1946–1947. The war had just ended, and 1946 was the first year for a football team at Reynoldsburg High. A robust marching band was a prerequisite to make formations on the field during halftime shows. This band incorporated members from the third grade through seniors in high school. From left to right are (first row, kneeling) Ardith Scott, Joan Holzbacher, Tommy Bertman, Sharon Damsel, Marilyn Van Hoose, and Barbara Finkle; (second row) Barbara Nance, Donn Moling, Joe Will, Connie Damsel, Harold Stone, Eileen Parsons, Virginia Heffner, JoAnne Gardner, Linn Brubaker, Nancy Nance, and Vicky Donahey; (third row) Mary Alice Moorehead, Ruth Morris, Bobby Jim Cobel, Earnest Moorehead, Donna McMillin, Bobby Brown, Wilma Wiswell, Nancy Gorey, Jack Kitzmiller, and Martha Jane McNaughten; (fourth row) Patricia Savage, Carole Donahey, Merle Hofmeister, Joan McMillin, Barbara Moore, Robert Kilkenny, Ruth Graham, Marjorie McCall, and Mary Alice Roshon; (fifth row) Jim Norris, Grace Graham, Glenn Miller, Jack Smith, Joe Dusi, Beverly Houghtby, Mary Ellen Barrett, Gwen Slack, and Bob Grahl. (Courtesy of RTHS.)

Five

Community Involvement

Biplane in the Tussing Fields, c. 1925. When a biplane landed in the field, it became a photo opportunity. After the picture was taken, the pilot offered everyone a plane ride. From left to right are Mrs. Hop Brooks, Agatha Alspaugh, Bernice Smith, Victor Smith (child), Len Tussing, Hop Brooks, Bill Alspaugh, Russell Tussing, Roger Tussing (child), Fred Feucht, Carl Smith, and unidentified. (Courtesy of Sylvia Tussing Hering.)

Reynoldsburg Baseball Club, 1921. The Reynoldsburg Baseball Club became the Eastern League season champions in 1921. Gathering for their group photograph are, from left to right, (first row) unidentified, Lawrence Myers, Red Graham, Lester Minor, Harry Hayes, two unidentified; (second row) Budd Slack, Art Allen, three unidentified, Ed Horton (wearing a tie), Dutch Pickering, and two unidentified. (Courtesy of Jack Kitzmiller.)

Minstrel Show Cast, 1955. The Minstrel Show was an annual event that the Lions Club initiated in 1951, and it ran strong for 10 years under the direction of Jane Spencer. It included the participation of practically everyone in town. During the 1950s, residents were either in the cast, making the costumes, working backstage, selling advertisements, or buying tickets to watch the show. (Courtesy of Mary Turner Stoots.)

The Reynoldsburg-Truro Historical Society. The historical society was founded in 1975. In June 1976, Ralph Connell offered use of the room above his hardware store for a rental fee of $1 per year. Volunteers operated the museum for more than a decade before the society decided to purchase land at the corner of Jackson Street and Broadwyn Drive in 1985. In January 1993, Thad Greene and Marissa Ong donated a house. After countless fundraisers, in October 1993, the house was moved from the five-point intersection at Livingston Avenue and State Route 256 to the current location at 1485 Jackson Street across from the Hannah J. Ashton School. Over several years, major renovations, and the addition of a storage barn, all of the artifacts were moved from the space above Connell's store to the new location, and the museum's doors opened in 2007. The purchase and restoration of the Bennett garage completed the three-building complex. (Courtesy of RTHS.)

JESSIE WHITE WEIBERG FORMS THE CIVIC CLUB. In 1922, Jesse White Weiberg (1880–1965) formed the Reynoldsburg Civic Club. The club bought and maintained the first traffic light; started the first library; established the first kindergarten; purchased the first flagpole for the municipal building; helped bring the Vietnam Moving Wall to Reynoldsburg; purchased large "Welcome to Reynoldsburg" signs and athletic equipment for the schools; sponsored Girl Scout troops; sent representatives to Buckeye Boys and Girls State; and gave funds to refurbish the middle school auditorium and to Helping Hands, the Cancer Fund, the Heart Fund, and United Appeals. The motto for the Reynoldsburg Civic Club is, "These Things We Will Do." The club is still in existence today and meets on the first Tuesday of the month from September through June. They can be contacted through the Reynoldsburg-Truro Historical Society. (Courtesy of Cornelia M. Parkinson.)

The First Tomato Festival Queen, 1966. Debra Lee Hutson was in the Reynoldsburg High School class of 1969. She was elected as the first Tomato Festival queen when the event began in 1966. During the parade, she rode in a car with Mayor George Twyford. Reynoldsburg lost a beautiful and kind lady when Hutson passed away in January 1977 at the age of 26. (Courtesy of RTHS.)

Virgil Raines, Scoutmaster. Raines is standing beside his 1937 Chevrolet. Raines organized the first Boy Scout troop in Reynoldsburg in the early 1930s. With advisors Aden Jones and Rex Whitehead, he took the troop camping in Hocking County, around Conkle's Hollow, which was then wild and remote. The experiences they shared—even for boys who had grown up in the fields and woods—were unforgettable. (Courtesy of Richard W. Parkinson.)

THE REYNOLDSBURG ROLLER RINK, 1964. The roller rink was built in the early 1960s, and on Saturday nights it was the place to be. The Reynoldsburg Roller Rink had a live band every weekend. During the week, people could take skating lessons, skate for fun, or even get into competitive skating, as shown in the above image (with Dianne Foltz Hoffman in the front of the line). Some of the contestants are shown below in no particular order. Their names were retrieved from a program from a competition held at the Coliseum in Mansfield, Ohio. They include Bucky Yahn, Kay Darby, Bob Hall, Dianne Foltz, Stu Martin, and Jackie Darby. (Both, courtesy of Dianne Foltz Hoffman.)

Fire Department, 1939. The 1939 Truro Township Volunteer Fire Department assembled for a photograph in front of their new fire station, which was built in 1938 primarily through donations of materials and labor. The total cost for the building was $687.85. Vinton H. Raymer (1905–1985) was the first chief of the Truro Township Volunteer Fire Department. From left to right are Neil Graham, Pete Ashton, George Compton, Bryant "Mickey" Slack, Bill Damsel, John Cobel, Rex Whitehead, Bert Ebright, Wally Hempstead, Jake Van Schoyck, Gib Barrett, Dan Compton, Harold Montgomery, John Schwartz, and Ez Stapleton; Chief Raymer is in the white hat and coat. The below photograph shows the building with the mounted siren used to summon the volunteer firemen. (Above, courtesy of RTHS; right, courtesy of George and Kendall Weeks.)

REYNOLDSBURG MAYORS 1840-2020

Years	Mayor	Years	Mayor
1840	Abraham Johnson	**1901**	J.M. Lindsay
1841-1843	Daniel Taft	**1902-1903**	John L. Oldham
1844	Robert Shield	**1904-1906**	C.H. Fishpaw
1845	Archibald Cooper	**1907-1909**	D.S. Evans
1846	James O'Kane	**1910-1920**	Claude Osborn
1847	Robert Shield	**1921**	David Murray Graham
1848-1852	No Borough Elections	**1922-1925**	Bryant "Mickey" Slack
1853	Robert Shield	**1926-1929**	C.W. Martin
1854-1855	J.B. West	**1930-1931**	Henry C. Smith
1856	Richard Rhoades	**1932-1933**	Walter Dressel
1857	J.B. West	**1934-1935**	F.B. "Doc" Poole
1858-1862	Mathew H. Rhoades	**1936-1941**	Henry K. Steckel
1863-1865	J.H. Miller	**1942**	Curtis P. Price
1866	Robert Trimble	**1943**	Wendell Fishpaw
1867-1868	John Schoonover	**1944-1945**	Ernest C. Brauning
1869-1871	A.J. Graham	**1946-1949**	Harold J. Stouder
1872	H. Wilson & W.W.Johnson	**1950-1951**	Bryant "Mickey" Slack
1873-1875	W.W. Johnson	**1952-1957**	Waldo Wollam
1876-1877	John H. Lynch	**1958-1959**	Harold J. Stouder
1878-1881	John B. West	**1960-1963**	Charles C. Lemert
1882-1883	Albert Casebancia Osborn	**1964-1971**	George W. Twyford
1884-1886	A.T. Graham	**1972-1979**	Richard Daugherty
1887	C.J. Hutson	**1980-1987**	John K. Francis
1888-1889	Hiram Dysart	**1988-2007**	Bob McPherson
1890-1898	E.S. Osborn	**2008-2019**	Brad McCloud
1899-1900	Fay May	**2020**	Joseph Begeny

REYNOLDSBURG MAYORS, 1840 TO 2020. Reynoldsburg became incorporated as a village on March 16, 1839. The first borough election was held in the fall of 1840, and voters elected Abraham Johnson the first mayor. The longest-term mayor was Bob McPherson, who served the city of Reynoldsburg for 19 years. (Courtesy of Cornelia M. Parkinson.)

CONNELL HARDWARE HOT STOVE LEAGUE, 1978. It was almost a daily sight to find these gentlemen gathered at the Connell Hardware Store and sharing the latest neighborhood news. Members of the Hot Stove League pictured here are, from left to right, Frank Rowland, Ralph Connell, Keith Seeds, William Vernon "Pete" Ashton, Ted Kibbey, Nelson Smith, and Earl Hart. (Courtesy of Charity Connell.)

JOHN MERRINGER, COURAGEOUS LIFESAVER. The Truro Township Trustees and Reynoldsburg Jaycees presented a special lifesaving award to John Merringer. Witnesses said that on June 23, 1969, while William (Bo) Merringer, 29, lay dead on one side of the creek, his brother, John, 24, was administering mouth-to-mouth resuscitation to David White, 45, on the other side. White was the only one of three rescuers to survive a plunge into the creek. "There is no question in my mind," said funeral home owner Perry "Pete" Rutherford, "that White would never have made it if it weren't for Johnny." Pete said that on the way to Lincoln Memorial Hospital, every time the ambulance hit a bump in the road, Dave White would spit out water. So, when Pete saw a bump, he ran over it. (Courtesy of Mary and John Merringer.)

Floodwaters in Paul Millar's Basement, 1956. The creeks in Reynoldsburg flood about every 100 years. After the rising water in Blacklick Creek and French Run flooded the area in 1956, the Truro Township Fire Department came to pump out the basement of Paul and Maebelle Millar's house. In the above photograph, a barefoot Maebelle stands behind the fire truck next to Paul. Pictured below are, from left to right, an unidentified *Columbus Dispatch* reporter-photographer, grandpa Wason Millar (kneeling), and David Nessley (standing where the basement wall collapsed). (Above, courtesy of Suzy Millar Miller; below, courtesy of Maebelle Millar.)

Bert Ebright, Truro Township and Village Constable. Ebright served as the Franklin County deputy sheriff for 55 years. For 38 of those years, he was also a constable in Truro, Marion, and Mifflin Townships. In those days, law officers provided their own transportation. When Ebright died on January 30, 1981, flags were flown at half-mast over the municipal building and the firehouse. (Courtesy of James O. Ruvoldt.)

The 1958–1959 Planning and Zoning Commission. Since the town's population had grown over 976 percent between 1950 and 1960, the members of this commission had their hands full. From left to right are (seated) Ralph Shively, Chuck Esterly, Hartl Lucks, Jim Pickering, and Richard Parkinson; (standing) Perry Walz (building inspector) and Mayor Harold "Jack" Stouder. (Courtesy of Cornelia M. Parkinson.)

French Run on Fire. On October 21, 1937, the creek caught on fire, but it was not spontaneous. A 6,500-gallon tanker truck had overturned on Main Street, and firemen washed the gasoline off the street and into the stream and sewers. An overpowering stink came into people's homes. This sparked the curiosity of King Pickering (1867–1958), who was the town character—he knew it and cultivated the appellation. He was often spotted telling stories to a group of boys fascinated by his tales. After a few days, the stink from the gasoline still saturated the air. Pickering wondered if there was still enough gasoline in the creek to burn. So, he tossed a lit newspaper into French Run. The resulting blaze was not doused by a heavy rain that was falling at the time, and it lasted some minutes. (Photograph by James O. Ruvoldt for the *Reynoldsburg Press*; courtesy of Cornelia M. Parkinson.)

Reynoldsburg Village Council, 1950s. The Village Council of Reynoldsburg is pictured in session. From left to right are (seated) Harold L. "Pick" Richardson, Floyd Powell, unidentified, Bob Francis, Jim Pickering, Harold J. Stouder, and Kay Clymer; (standing) Tom Walker, planning and zoning officer Perry Walz, and John Adams. (Courtesy of Rollan Powell.)

Wrestlers Big Bill Miller and Wild Bill Zim. On the left, Big Bill Miller (1927–1997) was a nine-time letterman at The Ohio State University, a three-time All American, and—later—a Reynoldsburg veterinarian. On the right, Wild Bill Zim (1913–1993) was also known as Zimovich, Buffalo Bill, and more. Zim learned bodybuilding and wrestling in the Marines and the circus. He was known for his long curly locks, comical rollicking performances, and artistic talent. (Courtesy of Mike Zim.)

1889 CENTENARY OF GEORGE WASHINGTON'S INAUGURATION. Students, teachers, and residents all joined Darlington J. Snyder to celebrate the 100-year anniversary of George Washington's inauguration, and Dr. Snyder's words were truly memorable. Dr. Snyder is the gentleman with the long beard standing in the center. The group posed in front of the town's largest building, the Reynoldsburg Union Academy. Several members of the crowd painted signs for this occasion. The signs read, from left to right, (first sign) "George Washington at Valley Forge—His Trust in God"; (second sign) "I swear, so help me God. George Washington at his first inauguration"; (third sign) the floral centerpiece over the door says, "From 1789 to 1889"; (fourth sign) "First in war; first in peace; and first in the hearts of his countrymen"; (fifth sign) "God, home, and native land." (Courtesy of RTHS.)

Knights of Pythias, Jasper Lodge No. 579, 1935. The Knights of Pythias was founded by Justus H. Rathbone in Washington, DC, on February 19, 1864. The Reynoldsburg Lodge stood next to the Masonic Lodge on Main Street. The lodge members purchased the building in 1890, and "K of P" remained on the front of the structure for over 100 years. (Courtesy of RTHS.)

Independent Order of Odd Fellows. This photograph came from Ralph Connell's collection and was donated by his daughter Charity. It appears to have been taken in the 1800s. These gentlemen belong to Lodge No. 411. The picture is not labeled, but the man standing to the right of the chair looks like David Benadum (1849–1928). (Courtesy of Charity Connell.)

THE INTERURBAN ELECTRIC RAILWAY. The Interurban Electric Railway operated in the early 20th century starting in 1902; it ended in late 1929 due to competition from buses, trucks, and cars. Reynoldsburg was connected to downtown Columbus by a rail network that transported passengers to Zanesville, Newark, Marion, Dublin, and Lancaster. The train tracks ran down the middle of Main Street. The cars carried passengers and some freight. A round-trip fare from Columbus was 35¢. The railway station in downtown Columbus employed several Reynoldsburg men. The below photograph shows the Interurban Freight House Force in May 1929. It includes Garry Wiswell (first row, third from the left) and his father, William Boyd Wiswell (first row, fifth from the left). (Above, courtesy of RTHS; below, courtesy of Mary Turner Stoots.).

Six

STREET SCENES AND LANDMARKS

MAIN STREET, 1890S. This view looks east on Main Street at Lancaster Avenue. Connell Hardware is on the right side of the photograph. The interurban tracks run down the center of the street, and the Masonic Lodge and Knights of Pythias buildings are on the left. (Courtesy of Cornelia M. Parkinson.)

Masonic Lodge and Knights of Pythias Buildings. The building on the left was the Masonic Hall. The Masons purchased the lot in 1882 and used the upper floor as their lodge and rented out the lower floor, which housed a drug and variety store for years (with many proprietors) until the early 1960s, when Wilma Dean Bryant and her husband, Tubby Dean, bought the building from the Masons. Wilma made living quarters upstairs and changed the name to The Village Store. It became Academy TV in the early 1970s, and "Kirby" sold metal detectors, slot machines, and beer steins. The Knights of Pythias purchased the building on the right in 1890 and made the upper floor into their lodge. In the 1940s, it was used as a grocery and housed thriving establishments until the buildings were destroyed on May 19, 2008. (Courtesy of RTHS.)

House Constructed with Stone from Forrester's Stone Quarry. This house was built in 1907 from stone quarried on Waggoner Road at Forrester's Stone Quarry. It was one of the earliest houses built in what would become the Highland Terrace addition north of Main Street on Lancaster Avenue. (Courtesy of Mary Turner Stoots.)

1937 Aerial View of Reynoldsburg. In 1937, the Reynoldsburg population was approximately 650. This aerial photograph faces southeast and was taken by James O. Ruvoldt (1903–1962), who was the owner and publisher of the *Reynoldsburg Press* from 1930 to 1941. The last road running from left to right at the top (on the east end of town) is Graham Road. (Courtesy of Margaret Devore Ruvoldt.)

The Bald Cypress. The bald cypress (*taxodium distichum*) is a native Southern tree and drops its needles annually. Since it was imported and is not indigenous to central Ohio, this type of tree does not normally survive the winters here, which designates this as one of the very few trees of its kind in Franklin County. This bald cypress was planted on the north side of Main Street by the Chamberlain family around 1880. The Chamberlains were butchers and owned quite a bit of land. The Reynoldsburg-Truro Historical Society placed a brass plaque at the foot of the tree in their honor over 40 years ago. (Both photographs by Mary Turner Stoots.)

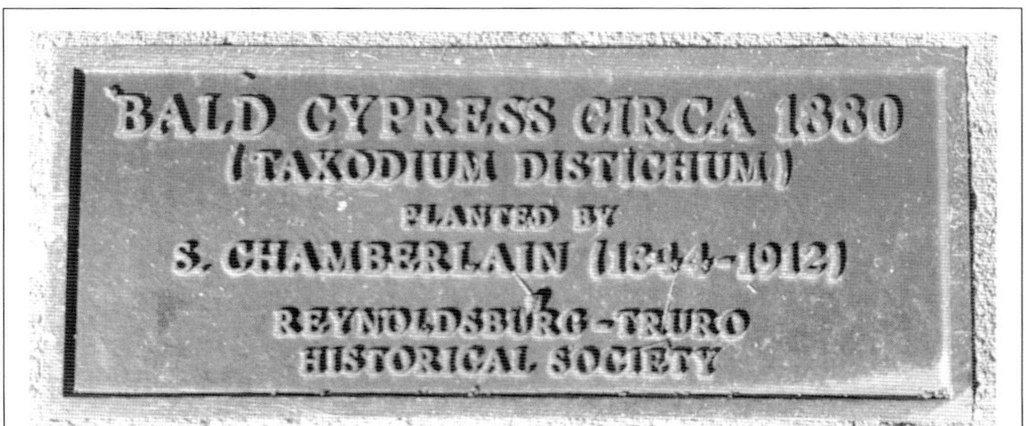

Grange Hall. This building was erected in 1927 as a "Portable School Building." The Reynoldsburg Grange met here until it was disbanded. There was a juvenile Grange in the basement. In the adult Grange, men sat on one side and women on the other. When the schoolhouse reached capacity in the early 1950s, elementary classes were held upstairs, while kindergarten was held in the basement. (Courtesy of Neal Piek.)

Reynoldsburg Post Office, 1956–1976. The Reynoldsburg population boom in the 1950s led to the initiation of door-to-door mail delivery, requiring a larger facility. Property was purchased at 7354 French Drive, formerly a coal yard. This post office was used for 20 years, until the town became too populated for such a small structure and the postal operation was moved to a former A&P Grocery building on Main Street. (Courtesy of Cornelia M. Parkinson.)

MURAL AT LANCASTER AND MAIN. This mural was painted by Curtis Goldstein. Work began on September 12, 2009, and started with a portrait of Hannah Ashton, one of the founding members of the Reynoldsburg-Truro Historical Society. The 90-by-30-foot mural, which depicts the history of Reynoldsburg and Ohio, is located on the west wall of Cotner Funeral Home in downtown Reynoldsburg. Upon completion, the mural was dedicated on December 5, 2009, during Christmas on the Towne Festivities. Included in the mural are five Reynoldsburg veterans: (in descending order) George Stebout, who died in Union service during the Civil War; 2nd Lt. Charles "Buddy" Feucht, who died in World War II; Sgt. Maebelle Weber, who served in World War II; Army specialist Robert "Ron" Buck, who was killed in Vietnam in February 1969; and Army sergeant Titus Reynolds, who was killed in Afghanistan in September 2009. (Courtesy of Mary Turner Stoots.)

The Alexander W. Livingston House. On his property, Livingston had many outbuildings that were excellent places for hiding people during daylight hours; this was important because his house was a stop on the Underground Railroad. The main house was built in 1864 or 1865 by Nathan Orcutt, a cabinetmaker by trade. Orcutt was the finest of workmen—strict about the exactness of fit between two pieces of wood, keeping a keen edge on his tools, and leveling horizontally and vertically as he built. Livingston is said to have paid an extra $1.50 per 1,000 board feet over the regular lumber price so he could select siding free of knots. When Orcutt was done, the Livingston house had a "furniture finish." Today, the house is a park and is rented out by the City of Reynoldsburg as a venue for tours and events. (Courtesy of Mary Turner Stoots.)

Lancaster Avenue Looking North from Main Street. This photograph shows Lancaster Avenue as a dirt road. On the far right is the stone house that sits on the corner of Lancaster Avenue and Rich Street; it was built around 1907 by William Forrester for Wilson Rush. This was one of the first houses built in Highland Terrace, the "New Addition." The house was sold to Henry and Ada Smith around 1920. There was no electricity in the house when the Smiths bought it. In 1922, electricity was brought into town for residential and business structures; Henry Smith had electric lines installed at that time. The two houses on the left side of the street were built by (house in front) Milton and Mary Kate Strahl and by (house in back) J.J. Enlows. Both houses are still standing, including the barn! This photograph is dated April 7, 1911. (Courtesy of RTHS.)

Seven

Agriculture and Business

Mickey Slack's Marathon Station. The Lower Tavern was demolished in 1932; Ohio Oil Company built a Linco station on the site, and it was operated by Bryant L. "Mickey" Slack. The station's name was later changed to Marathon. It was located on the northeast corner of Lancaster Avenue and Main Street. (Courtesy of Cornelia M. Parkinson.)

The Upper Tavern. On September 30, 1833, Benjamin Sells bought Lots 12 and 13 (site of the Upper Tavern) from John D. French. Sells gave a $2,600 mortgage to Nicholas Demerest. Reynoldsburg once had two major inns. This building has had numerous owners and has been home to a hotel, grocery, jewelry store, telephone office, beauty salon, private residence, interurban station, restaurant, and ice cream parlor. Jeweler Don Foltz bought the building in 1966, and during a remodel, he found a room below ground through a tunnel off the basement. It is believed that the room was used on the Underground Railroad. These photographs reflect some of the changes made under different proprietorships. (Above, courtesy of Margaret Ruvoldt; below, courtesy of Debbie Drerup Walterhouse.)

Wiswell's Market, the Red & White Store. Garry (1894–1968) and Maude (1899–1976) Wiswell opened a small grocery just eight days before the start of World War II in 1941. It was located at 7384 East Main Street and was called Wiswell's Market, the Red & White Store. It remained in operation for 21 years, until the arrival of Super Duper and Kroger in Reynoldsburg. Maebelle Millar worked for the Wiswells on and off for several years, but Wiswell's Market was primarily run by family, including Garry and Maude's daughter Wilma (Turner, 1929–2019), and son William "Bill" (1923–1985), who is pictured above with his father. Garry, Maude, and William are pictured below in 1924. (Both, courtesy of Mary Turner Stoots.)

Motz-Cook Grain Company. In 1890, Joseph Bigelow Powell built a grain elevator in Brice. In 1893, John H. Motz bought the elevator and began a business that served local farmers for the next 75 years. Partners in the business included members of the Motz, Hummell, Beery, and Cook families. Motz's primary partner was William Cook, the telegraph operator at the railroad depot across the tracks from the mill; Cook remained a partner until the 1930s. At the close of business in July 1967, Lester Motz had been with the firm for 53 years. Bookkeepers employed there included Orlie M. Cook, Ethel Schultis Boss, Fred Powell, Charles Walters, Esther VanGundy, and Anna Lee Herdman. Men who have worked there over the years include David Treher, George Mays, Eugene Lewis, Elmer and Curtis Petty, Dewey Finney, Webb Powell, and Dan Herdman. John Zarbaugh worked there for 43 consecutive years. (Courtesy of Dorothy Motz Evans.)

Forrester Limestone Quarry. In 1867, William A. Forrester (1841–1920), a Civil War veteran in his late twenties, reopened a quarry that had been worked for most of years between 1828 and 1854. Located on Waggoner Road, it was one of the largest blue freestone quarries in Ohio. Forrester employed several men who walked a mile or more to and from work each day. He used double sets of steam-powered saws and kept them constantly running. Two houses in Reynoldsburg were constructed of this tannish stone. The house pictured here was built in 1890. Forrester operated the quarry through at least 1909. During the 1930s, the State of Ohio Department of Conservation donated pine seedlings that were planted by teenager Richard W. Parkinson on the land, which was eventually donated to the city. The site of the quarry is now the Pine Quarry Park. (Courtesy of Cornelia M. Parkinson.)

The Connell Hardware Store. When its doors finally closed, the Connell Hardware Store ended 141 consecutive years of service to the Reynoldsburg community. Ezra Samuel Osborn established E.S. Osborn as a tin shop in 1872. Nelle was Ezra's daughter, and she married Elzy Connell. The tin shop moved several times, but in 1934, Elzy moved the business to Mason Hall, and it never was moved again. The building was constructed in 1883 and is one of the oldest business structures remaining in town today. When Nellie and Elzy's son Ralph received his honorable discharge, he came back to Reynoldsburg and ran the business until the day he died there in April 2007. For several years afterward, George "Cody" Lemaster operated the store with the help of Willard Carl. Cody became ill and died in May 2013, and Connell Hardware closed in August 2013. (Courtesy of RTHS and Cornelia M. Parkinson.)

C.W. Morris Packing Company. Reynoldsburg was once known as a meat town, with several packinghouses within the city limits. The C.W. Morris Packing Company was located on Truro Road on the east side of Blacklick Creek in old Reynoldsburg. Charles W. Morris's sons William "Nelson" Morris and James E. Morris both served in World War II. Nelson was a B-17 pilot for the US Army Air Forces, and James was in the US Navy. The slaughterhouse crew assembled in 1930 for a photograph; they are, from left to right, (first row, children) William "Nelson" Morris (1919–2001), James Elmore Morris (1924–2011), and Richard E. Morris (1926–1986); (second row) Warner Mix, Charles William Morris (owner), Frank Morris, Fred Morris, Cyril Oldham, and Floyd Powell; (third row) Ben Mildton, Jack Dillon, George Morse, Al Morse, Jack Morse, Dan Compton, Neil Cumler, and Tom Mix. (Courtesy of RTHS.)

The Reynoldsburg Bank. The Reynoldsburg Bank Company opened in 1904 and closed in 1930 due to the Great Depression. For the next 28 years, Reynoldsburg did not have a bank. In 1957, Dale England and Evan Williams gathered investors, and the bank opened on February 7, 1958, in a remodeled storeroom inside Connell Hardware. On opening day, 125 checking accounts, 79 savings accounts, and 13 Christmas Club accounts were opened. A new bank, erected in 1960, has a hyperbolic paraboloid roof. After more than 60 years, it is still the most architecturally interesting building in the city. The Reynoldsburg Bank became City National Bank in 1963, Bank One in 1979, and J.P. Morgan Chase Bank in 2006. (Both, courtesy of Carol England.)

The Investors Who Gave Reynoldsburg a Bank. In less than two years, starting on opening day in February 1958 with an initial capitalization of $200,000, the Reynoldsburg Bank's assets reached $4 million. In 1960, the bank built a new facility. The men responsible are pictured above; they are, from left to right, legal counsel Robert Teaford, director Dr. Herbert Ervin, president Evan Williams, president of City National Bank John G. McCoy, director Bernard D. Redman, director Byron Sabin, and vice president and cashier Dale England. Pictured below are early-1960s bank employees. From left to right are (first row) Frances Dorst, Chlotene Rausch, Shirley Cunningham, Jennie Warner, two unidentified, Ann Justice, Ann DeVito, Barbara Friesner, and Gloria Swarner; (second row) Pat Butler, Ruth Wood, Dale England, Wilford Williams, Frank Ayers Jr., Barbara Naayers, Phyllis Justice, Martha Donaldson, Vaneta Justus, and Carol Fritz. (Both, courtesy of Carol England.)

Don Foltz Jewelers. Don and Thelma Foltz moved to Reynoldsburg in 1950. After first working from home, Don opened his jewelry store in October 1953. He purchased the building in 1966. For the next 37 years, it was the only jewelry store in town. Don and Thelma's daughter Dianne worked in the store for 20 years. She is also a registered jeweler and certified gemologist with a certificate in jewelry design. Local residents bought all of their class rings, cuff links, anniversary presents, charms, Mother's Day presents, wedding rings, and much more from Don and Thelma. (Both, courtesy of Dianne Foltz Hoffman.)

Cotner Funeral Home. William "Bill" Cotner became a licensed funeral director in 1960 after graduating *summa cum laude* from the Cincinnati College of Mortuary Science. He worked in Columbus for 13 years before deciding to relocate to Reynoldsburg. In 1972, Cotner bought the P.E. Rutherford Funeral Home, and it has been Cotner Funeral Home ever since. Bill passed away in 2009, and his wife, Betty, died in 2012. Their son, Barth Cotner, graduated from the Cincinnati College of Mortuary Science in 1993, served his apprenticeship in 1994, and became a licensed funeral director in 1995. The Cotner business remains in the family. The houses converted to the funeral home were built around late 1800s and are conjoined. The complex is in the center of the historic district of Reynoldsburg. (Above, courtesy of William Cotner; below, courtesy of Lisa Long.)

WILLIAM VERNON ASHTON SR. FARM. Birdie Alice Green was born on Noe Bixby Road in 1869. She graduated from Reynoldsburg Union Academy in 1892 and taught school for nine years. In 1901, she married William Vernon Ashton, and later that year, she had twins, Hannah Jane and Joseph "Joe" Covert. The Will Ashton house and barn sat just over the Fairfield County line 1.5 miles south of Reynoldsburg. The barn was built around 1904, when Hannah and Joe were children. The house was built around 1898 by carpenter Al Myers. The house and outbuildings were torn down around 1966 to make way for the Interstate 70 entrance ramp off State Route 256. (Both, courtesy of Paul Moore.)

Eight

Notable People from Truro Township

MARY ANN ROCHELLE HICKMAN. Hickman is pictured in her kitchen at the age of 100. Born on November 15, 1837, she died on July 23, 1941. Mary Ann is believed to be the oldest person who has ever lived in Reynoldsburg. (Photograph by James O. Ruvoldt for the *Reynoldsburg Press*.)

Ralph Connell. Connell (1925–2007) was the third-generation owner of Connell Hardware and a pillar of the community. He was like family to those who grew up here or frequented his store. He loved fishing in Deer River, Minnesota. He was the past president of Silent Home Cemetery, past president of the Reynoldsburg-Truro Historical Society, and member of the Reynoldsburg Senior Citizens Center, Livingston House Society, and the United Methodist Church, where he served as an usher and was also a treasurer. Stationed in Hawaii, he served in the US Coast Guard for three years during World War II. He was a 59-year member Past Master of the Reynoldsburg Lodge 340 Free and Accepted Masons, secretary for 25 years, Past High Priest Walnut Chapter 172 Royal Arch Masons, Past Illustrious Master Columbus Council 8 Royal and Select Masters, Mount Vernon Commandery 1 Knights Templar, Scottish Rite Valley of Columbus, Aladdin Temple Shrine, and 51-year member and Past Worthy Patron Eugenie Chapter 507 Order of the Eastern Star. (Courtesy of Charity Connell and RTHS.)

Jo Ann Davidson, Speaker of the House. Davidson was born in Findlay, Ohio, in 1927. She settled in Reynoldsburg, where she raised her family and embarked on her political career in 1967, when she was elected to Reynoldsburg City Council. She always served with distinction. In 1977, she was elected to the office of Truro Township Clerk. In 1980, Davidson was elected to the Ohio House of Representatives and served as House Minority Leader in the 120th General Assembly. In 1995, she was selected as the first female speaker of the Ohio House of Representatives, a position in which she served until her term was up in 2001. Davidson continued to serve Ohio on a variety of boards and charity organizations. During her many years of service, she has served her state and community with dedication and distinction, led by example, and earned the deep respect and gratitude of the many individuals she has represented. (Courtesy of the Jo Ann Davidson Ohio Leadership Institute.)

Hometown Hero Robert Ronald "Ronnie" Buck. Specialist IV Robert Ronald Buck (1946–1969) was posthumously awarded the Silver Star for gallantry in action, Bronze Star Medal, Purple Heart, and Good Conduct Medal after he was killed in action in Vietnam on February 23, 1969. Buck had previously been awarded the National Defense Service Medal, Vietnam Service Medal, Vietnam Campaign Ribbon, Combat Infantryman Badge, Expert Badge with rifle bar, and the Marksman Badge with automatic rifle bar. He was a 1965 graduate of Reynoldsburg High School, where he earned a varsity letter in baseball. He attended Columbus Business College for two years, majoring in business administration, followed by working at Corrugated Container Company before he was drafted into the Army in May 1968. The following February, he suffered fatal combat wounds. (Left, courtesy of Shirley Buck; below, courtesy of Vicki Buck Rollins.)

MELVIN FUNK, ARTIST AND CARTOONIST. Melvin Funk (1914–1997) graduated from Reynoldsburg High School in 1933. He signed all his artwork with "Funk"—it was not until a handmade greeting card was sent to Hannah Ashton that his first name was revealed. One of his drawings was published in an Army magazine, the *Hawaiian Defender*. His cartoons could be from a master *New Yorker* cartoonist rather than a teenage artist. The drawings are reflective of a time in the city's history when high school basketball, baseball, and speedball (football did not reach Reynoldsburg until 1946) were a much bigger part of the fabric of the town, with long ticket lines extending out the doors of the Jackson Street school on game nights. There was no ESPN to keep sports fans at home in those days. (Both, courtesy of RTHS.)

John Joseph "Jack" Godfrey, Survivor. Many folks in Reynoldsburg remember Jack Godfrey (1921–2008) as partner-owner of the *Little Weekly*, the hometown newspaper. Jack and his wife, Irene (1919–2013), got married in 1944 and moved to Reynoldsburg in 1956. Most people were unaware of Jack's military experiences. He had been a prisoner of war during World War II after being shot down in a B-24 Liberator four-engine heavy bomber. He was held prisoner by the Germans for nine months, ending in a 500-mile death march during the worst winter in that area for 50 years—8,000 men started the march, but only 5,000 finished. All 10 of the aircraft crew were taken prisoner by the Germans. Jack Godfrey came home. All of the crewmen survived and met annually until ill health or death prevented it. At his last reunion, Jack was 85. (Courtesy of Margi Godfrey Sawyer.)

WILLIAM "FRED" GRAHAM, PHD. Graham (1930–2021) was a retired professor, a minister, an author, a speaker, a teacher, a husband, a father, and an all-around good man. He was a person to be respected in every way. He graduated from Reynoldsburg High School in 1948, where he was very active in sports. He was a lifelong baseball fan. He went to Tarkio College in Missouri, earning his bachelor's degree, then to the Pittsburgh Seminary. He received his PhD from the State University of Iowa. In 1953, he married Jean Garrett, and they had four daughters. His accomplishments include serving as emeritus professor at Michigan State University in East Lansing (instructor, 1963–1964; assistant professor, 1964–1969; associate professor, 1969–1973; professor, 1973–1992). Fred was an ordained Presbyterian minister and pastor of the Bethel United Presbyterian Church, Waterloo, Iowa, from 1955 to 1961. Fred was also president of the Sixteenth-Century Studies Society in 1988 and 1989. Dr. Graham's publications include *The Constructive Revolutionary: John Calvin and His Socio-Economic Impact*, 1971; *Picking Up the Pieces: A Christian Stance in a Godless Age*, 1975; and (as editor) *Later Calvinism: International Perspectives*, 1994. (Courtesy of Grace Graham Tanner and RTHS.)

Dr. Jesse Johnson. Dr. Johnson (1863–1951) was a devout and learned man. He held degrees as a doctor of divinity and doctor of laws. He graduated with the first class of Reynoldsburg High School in 1882 and from Allegheny Seminary in 1894, then served as president of Muskingum College for 10 years. In honor of his highly successful administration, that college's Johnson Hall is named in tribute to him. As a young man, he was a missionary to Egypt and would show off his watch fob shaped like a sarcophagus with a tiny "mummy" inside. From 1903 to 1930, he held the elected post of professor of church history and apologetics at Xenia Seminary. Proficient in Greek, he taught some classes in it; he also took a correspondence course in Hebrew. For nine years, he held a pastorate at Mt. Ayr, Iowa, retiring to Reynoldsburg in 1939. (Courtesy of Cornelia M. Parkinson.)

Al Haft. Haft (1886–1976) was a wrestler (professional and amateur), Ohio State wrestling coach (from 1920 to 1925), and prominent wrestling and boxing promoter (from 1914 to 1965). He brought many greats to Reynoldsburg, including boxers "Gentleman" Jim Corbett, Jack Dempsey, Primo Carnera, and Joe Louis, and wrestlers "Strangler" Lewis, Chief Don Eagle, Gorgeous George, and "Nature Boy" Buddy Rogers. In 1948, Haft helped organize the National Wrestling Alliance, a predecessor of the WWE (World Wrestling Entertainment, Inc.). He established the first televised wrestling match in Columbus in 1950 but discontinued it after a few months, thinking it would reduce live show attendance. He raised horses and turkeys at his Reynoldsburg farm and staged outdoor wrestling shows there. Around 1957, he sold 250 acres to Huber Homes, and by 1958, the company had built 300 ranch homes. (Right, courtesy of Mike Zim; below, courtesy of Regina Haft.)

ALEXANDER W. LIVINGSTON. Although tomatoes had been cultivated to various degrees throughout the world, it was Livingston and his seed company that contributed more than any other to development of the tomato. When Livingston began his attempts to develop the tomato as a commercial crop, his goal was to produce tomatoes that were smooth-skinned, uniform in size, and had better flavor. After many attempts at hybridization, he instead began a process of selecting seeds from tomato plants exhibiting specific characteristics. Through this selection process, he discovered a plant that bore perfect tomatoes like its parent vine. After 20 years of selection, the fruit became fleshier and larger. In 1870, he introduced the Paragon. Prior to his work, tomatoes were commonly ribbed, had hard cores, and were generally a hollow fruit. In all, the Livingston Seed Company introduced 31 varieties of tomatoes. (Courtesy of Cornelia M. Parkinson and RTHS.)

David Leigh McConagha. In 1964, David Leigh McConagha (1941–2019) embarked on a 27-year naval career featuring more than 25 years of flight experience with bomber aircraft. He taught at the US Naval Academy Preparatory School and the Naval Training Center in Bainbridge, and he did flight training at two different schools. He flew reconnaissance in Vietnam and was an ROTC instructor at Dartmouth College while earning his master's degree. He did tours on the aircraft carriers *Saratoga* and *Dwight D. Eisenhower.* In 1983, he was transferred to the Pentagon, where he worked in the offices of the chief of naval operations, director for operations, and joint staff. After retirement, he served as the director of the office of weapons surety. In the international arena, he contributed to both the North Atlantic Treaty Organization (NATO) nuclear weapons safety and security programs and cooperative surety efforts with the United Kingdom. (Courtesy of Carolyn Kreider Egner.)

Harold Schenk and Bo Merringer. A Little League baseball coach and helpful neighbor drowned on June 23, 1969, in a rain-swollen Blacklick Creek in Reynoldsburg moments after saving the life of a 10-year-old boy who had fallen in the creek. The victims were identified as (on the left) Harold G. Schenk, 39, and (on the right) William "Bo" Joseph Merringer, 29. Both were pronounced dead at the scene after being pulled from the water by rescuers and the Reynoldsburg Fire Department. A third man, who also helped rescue the boy, was pulled unconscious from the water and revived. He was identified as David T. White Sr., 45. Eyewitness Tim Pfautsch, 17, a worker for the Reynoldsburg Recreation Department, said he heard women and children screaming and ran to the rescue. He started to walk across the dam along the upper edge. About a third of the way across, he fell in, and an unidentified man pulled Tim to the side and saved his life. (Courtesy of Suzy Millar Miller, RTHS, and the Schenk family.)

Maebelle L. Weber Millar. Born and raised in Truro Township, Maebelle Weber (1920–1998) graduated from Reynoldsburg High School in 1938 and was one of four Reynoldsburg women to serve in the military during World War II. In 1943, she answered the call to duty and enlisted in the Women's Army Auxiliary Corps (WAAC), reporting for duty at Fort Hayes in Columbus before being shipped to her first duty station in Daytona Beach, Florida. While at Daytona, she attended non-commissioned officers' school and became a first platoon sergeant after only one month in the service. Her primary jobs at Daytona were as a drill master and physical training instructor. After Daytona, she was assigned to the Army Airways Communications Service (AACS) at Godman Field in Fort Knox, Kentucky, where she went to Radio Control Tower School to become a tower operator. She served in the Army for three years and fourteen days, and according to a note she wrote, "I loved it all." (Courtesy of Suzy Millar Miller.)

Cpl. Lindsay William Mitchell. Mitchell (1927–1951) graduated from Reynoldsburg High School with the class of 1945. (Lindsay's older sister Mae, a 1943 graduate of Reynoldsburg High School, became a very successful businesswoman.) After high school, Lindsay enlisted in the US Army and served with honor during the Korean War. He held the rank of corporal, and his military occupation or specialty was heavy weapons infantryman. He was attached to the Fifth Cavalry Regiment, First Cavalry Division. Corporal Mitchell was killed in action at the age of 24 while fighting in North Korea at the battle zone of the Chorwon area on October 29, 1951. His commendations include Purple Heart, Combat Infantryman Badge, Korean Service Medal, National Defense Service Medal, Republic of Korea Presidential Citation, Republic of Korea War Service Medal, United Nations Service Medal, Army Presidential Unit Citation, and the Army Good Conduct Medal. (Portrait by Colin Sutphin; courtesy of RTHS.)

James Whitney Near, the Hamburger Prodigy. Near (1938–1996) graduated from Reynoldsburg High School in 1956. He began flipping burgers at the Burger Boy Mainliner Restaurant in Berwick at the age of 15. After school, he walked to Livingston Avenue and hitchhiked or walked the seven miles to work. After he graduated from high school, he became the night manager at Burger Boy, then went to Hanover College in Indiana. He graduated from Hanover in 1960, then did a short stint in the Ohio National Guard. His former boss at Burger Boy cofounded Burger Boy Food-o-Rama (BBF) and invited Near to become a manager, then vice president of the new chain. Borden bought out BBF, and Near was named president of Borden Retail Operations. When his Borden contract ran out, Jim invested in Wendy's franchises and opened 39 restaurants. Eventually, he was named CEO and chairman of Wendy's International. Pictured here are Dave Thomas (seated at left); Bob Barney, CEO (seated at right); and Near, president of Wendy's. (Courtesy of Dan Near.)

Author Cornelia M. Parkinson. Born in Casey, Illinois, Connie McNary came to Reynoldsburg in 1941. She is a 1943 graduate of Reynoldsburg High School. In 1944, she married Richard W. Parkinson, vice chairman and professor of engineering graphics at The Ohio State University. Their daughters are Cassandra (married Owen E. Adams Jr.), Claudia Parkinson, and Cornelia (married Jeffrey J. Iles). In 1956 and 1957, Connie was the Reynoldsburg Presbyterian Church secretary. From 1958 to 1962, she was secretary to Robert P. Heischman, executive head of Reynoldsburg Schools. Since 1966, she has been a professional writer, selling articles, short stories, brochures, books, and more. As Day Taylor, she is the coauthor of two best-selling paperback historical novels. *The Black Swan* was on the *New York Times* Best Seller List for 10 weeks, and *Mossrose* was the sequel. In 1981, Cornelia wrote the *History of Reynoldsburg and Truro Township, Ohio*, which is currently used in local schoolrooms. She has been published in several countries and is still writing. (Courtesy of Cornelia M. Parkinson and RTHS.)

William G. Pengelly. Pengelly (1865–1935) was one of the earliest authorities in the United States to recognize the study of documents and chirography (art of writing or engraving) as a nearly exact science demanding thorough study of the elements. Factors involved in handwriting analysis include use of the microscope and comparative signatures in determining true or forged handwriting; the documents themselves, and their age, composition of the paper, etc. Born in Plymouth, England, in 1865, and the son of a British Navy warrant officer, Pengelly came to this area in 1883. From then until 1915, he was employed by the Capital City Bank of Columbus, rising from secretary to president. As a banker, he became interested in fraudulent documents and pursued that study for many years; he was ranked among the foremost experts. The illustration portrays Pengelly as he would have looked in 1915. (Illustration by Colin Sutphin; courtesy of Cornelia M. Parkinson.)

Judge David Franklin Pugh. At the age of 16, Pugh (1845–1928) enlisted during the Civil War, serving in the 46th Regiment of the Ohio Volunteer Infantry. After the war, he attended The Ohio State University, and he was admitted to the bar in 1870. David married Ida Swan (1847–1928) in 1869. He served as a prosecuting attorney in Tyler County, West Virginia, for 10 years, representing that county at that state's Constitutional Convention in 1872. He was also a member of the legislature from Tyler County for one term. David and Ida then returned to Columbus, where David continued to practice law and was an instructor of equity at Ohio State University. David was appointed common pleas judge by Gov. Joseph B. Foraker in 1887. He was then elected in 1888 and reelected in 1893. (Courtesy of Cornelia M. Parkinson.)

Charles Frederick "Buddy" Feucht, Missing in Action. Charles Frederick Feucht (1918–1943) was raised in Reynoldsburg. Growing up, he was active in Boy Scouts, 4-H, and Juvenile Grange. In October 1939, he enlisted in the Ohio National Guard and was assigned to the 37th Division. Upon the United States entering into World War II, he transferred to the US Army Air Corps, was commissioned a second lieutenant, and received his bombardier wings. He disappeared when his plane went down. The crash was discovered high in the Sarawaget Range in Morobe Province in New Guinea. The clock in the bomber shows that it crashed at 1:21, one minute after its last radio call. Feucht's remains were not discovered for 59 years. He was finally laid to rest back home after 63 years on May 13, 2006. He was awarded the Purple Heart, Air Medal with Oak Leaf Cluster, Asia Pacific Campaign Medal with two stars, World War II Victory Medal, and the Ohio Distinguished Service Medal. (Courtesy of RTHS.)

Eleanor Wilson Shonting. A 1941 graduate of Reynoldsburg High School, Eleanor Mae Wilson (1924–2019) was an attractive teenager who loved to dance. As the only child of James Henry Wilson and Lola Blanche McNaghten Wilson Wright and a granddaughter of Blanche Holcomb and Stewart McNaghten, her roots in Truro Township date back to the late 1700s. Growing up, Eleanor was fascinated by family history and started to collect information and artifacts as early as she can remember. Since she was an only child, relatives naturally handed everything down to her. Even if they did not, she hunted down items or asked for a copy. Eleanor was an expert on photography and its development, as well as gravestones. She was a walking encyclopedia on both subjects and gave classes on them. As she was moved to an assisted-living facility, her lifelong collection of genealogy and artifacts was donated to the Reynoldsburg-Truro Historical Society. With over 300 binders of information, the McNaghten Collection is probably one of the largest and most professionally researched single genealogy collections in Central Ohio. (Courtesy of Eleanor Wilson Shonting and RTHS.)

BRYANT "MICKEY" SLACK. Bryant Slack (1900–1967) was the owner of the local Marathon station at the corner of Lancaster Avenue and Main Street. Slack was a 1922 graduate of Reynoldsburg High School, and he also enlisted and fought in two World Wars. He enlisted for the first time at age 17 during World War 1. His assignment was in Battery A 136 Field Artillery to discharge; Private Defensive Sector of the American Expeditionary Forces June 28, 1918, to March 24, 1919, with an honorable discharge April 10, 1919. After that war, he came home and finished high school, graduating at the age of 22. During World War II, he enlisted at age 41. He was a staff sergeant in the US Army Quartermaster 1590th Service Unit from November 14, 1942, until he was honorably discharged on August 21, 1943. (Courtesy of RTHS.)

GEORGE J. STEBOUT. According to an April 22, 1863, article in the *Ohio Statesman* newspaper, at the age of 20, Stebout (1843–1865) ran for the office of council member for the Reynoldsburg Village Council. He did not win the election, so he enlisted in the Army on September 1, 1863. He fought for the Union during the Civil War in Company F, the Fifth US Colored Troops Infantry, Sly-Tee. When the Reynoldsburg mural was painted, the historical society and Barth Cotner decided to include a picture of Stebout to represent the Civil War veteran. Stebout (seated in front, left of center) died during the war in 1865 and is buried in a marked grave in Seceder Cemetery along with three other Civil War soldiers: Wallace Graham, Roette McCullough, and John Taylor. (Courtesy of Cornelia M. Parkinson and Mary Turner Stoots.)

ZELLA TAYLOR, THE VILLAGE PIANO TEACHER. Zella E. Taylor (1889–1969) taught piano lessons for over 50 years to three generations of Reynoldsburg children. It is fascinating that the same woman who taught parents, aunts, and uncles how to play the piano in the 1930s could be teaching the same songs and notes to their descendants in the 1960s. Comparing the notebooks brought to each class, there was little variation in the notations from 1934 to 1962. Taylor stressed posture at the piano and finger curvature. All students learned to play children's music first, then graduated to simplified classical pieces. Taylor was meticulous in putting notes in the practice music. Almost every page had the beat count for each note, such as "1-2-3" or "1&2&3&4." Taylor shared half a double house with her sister Georgia Bell Taylor Headley (1880–1980). They were the daughters of Frank Gaylord Taylor and Mary Ellen Tusing. This photograph shows sisters Georgia, Floris (Condon, 1884–1962), and Zella Taylor around 1901. (Courtesy of Trish Otto and Suzy Millar Miller.)

Virginia Marie Williams, Air Force Pilot. Virginia Williams (1921–1999) played the processional at her Reynoldsburg High School graduation in 1939 and went on to attend the Conservatory of Music at Capital University. At the same time, unbeknownst to her parents, she joined the Civil Air Patrol and started taking flying lessons. On December 7, 1941, she heard about Pearl Harbor over the radio and rushed to the Sullivant Avenue Airfield with a new urgency. In 1941, over 25,000 people applied for the WASP (Women Airforce Service Pilots) program; 1,800 were chosen, with only 1,000 graduating from the rigorous seven-month course. One of those women was Virginia. WASP pilots ferried planes from coast to coast, transported military goods, and towed targets for gunnery practice, among other duties, freeing up male pilots for overseas combat. Thirty-eight WASP were lost in aircraft accidents. After the war, Virginia married Carroll Hubbard. In 2010, the 200 surviving WASPs were each presented with the Congressional Gold Medal. Virginia passed away in August 1999, but she posthumously received a Congressional Gold Medal that was presented to her family. (Courtesy of RTHS.)

Loren Gregory Windom. Loren Windom (1905–1988) served as adjutant general of the Ohio National Guard and retired as a major general. He was a former assistant United States attorney in the Southern District of Ohio and was the youngest member of the 37th's general staff. His awards include a Purple Heart with Oak Leaf Cluster, the Legion of Merit, the Combat Infantryman Badge, the Silver Star, the Bronze Star Medal, and the Distinguished Service Cross. After retirement, he continued to enjoy his hobby of amateur radio and was often spotted around his three 80-foot antennas in the back of his home. At one time, he was ranked as the No. 3 radio amateur in the world. He wrote extensively on the hobby and even invented an antenna, the Windom Antenna, which remains popular around the world. (Courtesy of David Windom.)

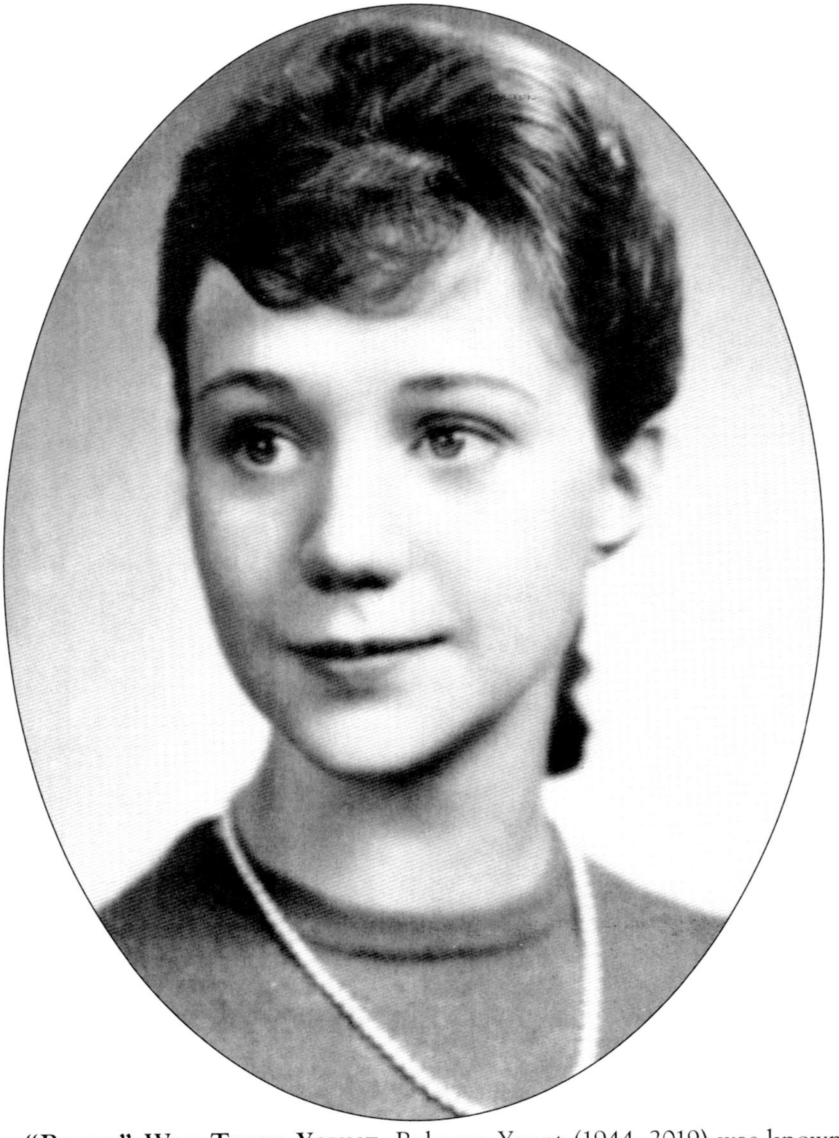

Rebecca "Becky" Way Tobin Yount. Rebecca Yount (1944–2019) was known for her series of crime novels featuring Scotland Yard inspector Michael "Mick" Chandra, as well as a Facebook series on home cooking entitled *Crime and Cottage Pie* and historical novels set in England. She was the daughter of teacher Nelle McCoy and journalist Dallas R. Tobin. She began music studies in conservatory at age eight, aiming toward a career as a concert pianist. As an undergraduate at Capital University, she had already published poetry and coedited the campus poetry magazine. Later, she wrote music and verse for voice, including "Three Songs of Transition," which was performed at Lincoln Center in New York. In conjunction with the US Department of Education and Bureau of the Census, she created the first comprehensive map of the nation's school boundaries. She also directed a nationwide program to invest private funds to strengthen America's public schools. In the 1980s, she drafted education legislation for Congress that became public policy. She was personally honored by grants from the Exxon Education Foundation and the Rockefeller Foundation. (Courtesy of RTHS.)

ABOUT THE REYNOLDSBURG-TRURO HISTORICAL SOCIETY. For over 45 years, the Reynoldsburg-Truro Historical Society has been owned by the members and operated by volunteers. We fund our organization entirely through donations, fundraisers, and dues. Our museum is our pride. Local history is a State of Ohio curriculum requirement for every third-grade student. Some of the society's most successful and rewarding activities include the spring and fall tours we host for every third-grader in the Reynoldsburg City School System. During the pandemic of 2020 and 2021, our museum was closed, but the children, teachers, and public were able to visit our facility complex through virtual tours filmed at the museum and accessible on our website at www.RTHS.info. Our goal is to educate every child on their heritage and the history of this town. Communication and collaboration with the public, school administrators, township trustees, and Reynoldsburg city officials are the keys to our success today and going forward. —Mary Turner Stoots, president of the Reynoldsburg-Truro Historical Society

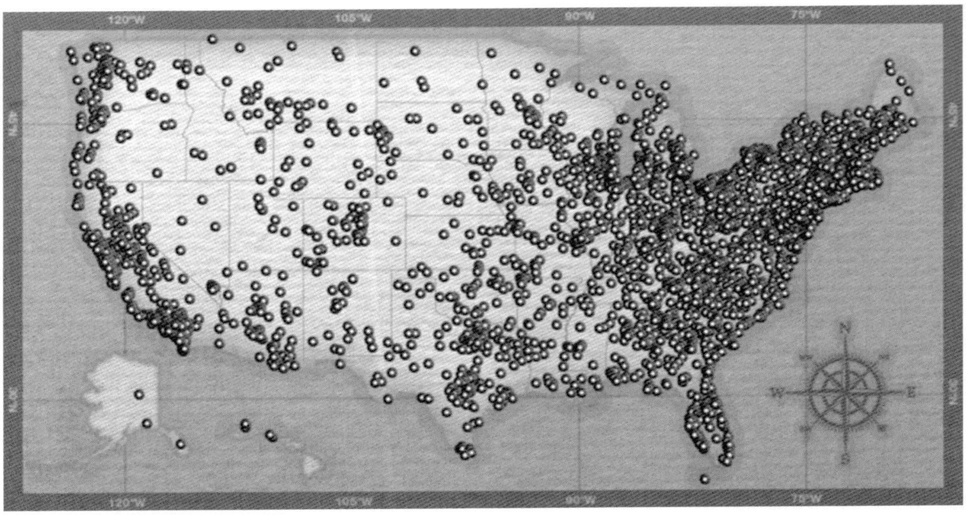

Consistent with our mission to preserve history on a local level, this book was printed in South Carolina on American-made paper and manufactured entirely in the United States. Products carrying the accredited Forest Stewardship Council (FSC) label are printed on 100 percent FSC-certified paper.

MADE IN THE USA